Princess Alice
1843–1878
m. Louis IV, Grand Duke of Hesse (d.1892)

[...]ers

Princess Victoria
1863–1950
m. Prince Louis of Battenburg, later 1st Marquess of Milford Haven (d.1921)

2 brothers and 4 sisters

Princess Alice
1885–1969
m. Prince Andrew of Greece (d.1944)

2 brothers and 1 sister

Henry,
Duke of Gloucester
1900–1974
m. Lady Alice Montagu-
Douglas-Scott

George,
Duke of Kent
1902–1942
m. Princess Marina
of Greece (d.1968)

Prince John
1905–1919

Philip,
DUKE OF EDINBURGH
b. 1921
m. Princess Elizabeth
(**QUEEN ELIZABETH II**)

4 sisters

Edward,
Duke of Kent
b. 1935
m. Katharine Worsley

Princess Alexandra
b. 1936
m. Hon. Angus Ogilvy

Prince Michael
b. 1942
m. Baroness Marie-
Christine von Reibnitz

George,
Earl of St Andrews
b. 1962
m. Sylvana Tomaselli

**Lady Helen
Windsor**
b. 1964
m. Timothy Taylor

**Lord Nicholas
Windsor**
b. 1970

James Ogilvy
b. 1964
m. Julia Rawlinson

Marina Ogilvy
b. 1966
m. Paul Mowatt
(divorced 1997)

**Lord Frederick
Windsor**
b. 1979

**Lady Gabriella
Windsor**
b. 1981

Columbus Taylor
b. 1994

Cassius Taylor
b. 1996

Flora Ogilvy
b. 1994

Alexander Ogilvy
b. 1996

Zenouska Mowatt
b. 1990

Christian Mowatt
b. 1993

Edward,
Baron Downpatrick
b. 1988

Lady Marina Windsor
b.1992

Lady Amelia Windsor
b.1996

Prince William
1941–1972

Richard,
Duke of Gloucester
b. 1944
m. Brigitte van Deurs

Alexander,
Earl of Ulster
b. 1974

Lady Davina Windsor
b. 1977

Lady Rose Windsor
b. 1980

THE QUEEN

50 years –
a celebration

RONALD ALLISON

Grafton

THE
QUEEN

50 years –
a celebration

RONALD ALLISON

Grafton

This edition produced for DMG Ltd in 2002.
First published in 2001 by HarperCollins*Publishers*
77-85 Fulham Palace Road
London W6 8JB.

Text copyright © Ronald Allison 2001

Ronald Allison reserves the moral right to be
identified as the author of the Work.

Layout designer: Penny Dawes
Indexer: Susan Bosanko

A catalogue record for this book is available from
the British Library.

ISBN 0 00 765005 1

Colour origination by Digital Imaging

Printed in Spain by Gráficas Estella.

DEDICATION

For my son David
and grandchildren Ross and Amadea
and in loving memory of my
grandson Tom

ACKNOWLEDGEMENTS

For five years during the 1970s I had the great good fortune to be the Press Secretary to Her Majesty The Queen. Before that I was the BBC's Court Correspondent and since my time at the Palace I have regularly written and broadcast about the Queen and the royal family. Those years and the experiences they brought have confirmed me as a staunch supporter of the monarchy and as a fervent admirer of the Queen herself. Indeed, it is my hope that this book will be seen as a tribute to Her Majesty and as an appropriate contribution to the celebrations of the golden jubilee. The years since 1952 have been truly remarkable ones for the United Kingdom and the Commonwealth, and it has been enormously to the benefit of both to have had the Queen at their head throughout that time.

I owe great debts of gratitude to those who, both knowingly and unwittingly, have helped with this book. The fact that the Queen's reign more or less coincided with the second half of the 20th century meant that some of the basic factual research I might otherwise have been obliged to carry out was in fact done for me by those chronicling the century. The millennium was, to me at least, well worth celebrating. I am grateful to all those who recorded the events of the 1900s.

My particular thanks go to Tom Corby, a former Court Correspondent for the Press Association, who opened up his files for me, and to those in the Buckingham Palace Press Office and in the Library at Windsor Castle who were, as ever, so helpful. The book, however, is in no sense an 'authorised' publication, although I hope it is both accurate and informed. Any opinions that filter through are mine unless otherwise attributed.

The book was commissioned when Eddie Bell was the Chief Executive Officer of HarperCollins, and others who were in the company and to whom I am deeply indebted include Polly Powell and Barbara Dixon. Caroline Taylor was a most marvellous editor, patient, insightful and an absolute stickler for accuracy – thank goodness. My thanks to Hilary Clarke and her flying fingers. I still call it typing – Hilary simply processes, accurately and amazingly quickly. At home my wife, Jennifer, was ever the encourager and the enabler – wonderfully helpful at all times.

Finally, I am deeply grateful to Her Majesty and His Royal Highness for allowing me to reproduce some of the Christmas cards they have sent over the past 50 years.

CONTENTS

INTRODUCTION

'I declare before you all that my whole life, whether it be long or short, shall be devoted to your service and the service of the great imperial family to which we all belong.'

$\mathcal{B}$roadcasting from South Africa to the Commonwealth and Empire on her 21st birthday on 26 April 1947, Princess Elizabeth made in this way her 'solemn act of dedication'. For someone older, more experienced, and wiser it would be an awesome undertaking; from one only just, officially, an adult it could have seemed a presumptuous, unrealistic pledge. But the Princess had a maturity beyond her years. Her character, her priorities, her sense of honour and of duty, and her appreciation of her position were already well established, and her declaration, in a less cynical age than our own, was taken at face value. And with what justification!

Since then, as Princess for less than five more years, but as Queen now for 50, Elizabeth II had been at her peoples' service through times of change as dramatic as any period in recorded history. She has 'reigned but not ruled', but has nevertheless led and represented her peoples with a consistent and sure touch that draws and deserves worldwide admiration. She has maintained an absolutely clear understanding of her role and is still, as she declared herself to be in 1947 and again in 1952, at the nation's service. She has kept faith in every sense of the word and is indeed a 'constant queen'.

The country to which she returned from Kenya as Queen on a cold February morning in 1952 was vastly different from the United Kingdom of today. It was an age of pounds, shillings and pence, of *Picture Post* and the Home Service. Petrol rationing had ended but roads were still clogged by cyclists rather than motorists. Children went to the local grammar school if they had passed their 'eleven plus',

OPPOSITE *The Coronation Service over, the Queen wore the Imperial State Crown for the journey from Westminster Abbey back to Buckingham Palace.*

or to the secondary modern if they had not. The vast majority of men had either served in the armed forces during the Second World War (1939–45), or would be called up for a two-year stint of national service. It was in theory a 'post-war' period but British soldiers and national servicemen were involved in bloody fighting in the Korean war, many others were to be fired on in anger in Kenya, Cyprus and elsewhere, and the Cold War with the USSR was to cast a pall of fear over the West for many years.

There was almost full employment, and comparatively few married women went out to work. The homes they ran had few of the resources now taken for granted. Washing machines and refrigerators were still only available for the better-off; central heating was a rarity; and there could hardly have been an air-conditioned building in the entire country.

The coalman called regularly, as did the milkman, the fishmonger, the greengrocer, the butcher, the baker and the ironmonger (ironmongers' vans were still, in the country, sometimes horse-drawn). The first self-service shop had opened in Croydon in 1950, but, although on its way, supermarket shopping was available to only a very few. In any case, choice was extremely limited; the austerity years were certainly not over yet.

Entertainment consisted of 'going to the pictures' or the palais de danse on a Saturday night, listening to the wireless (BBC only unless you could pick up Radio Luxembourg or a continental station), reading, or playing 78 rpm records of classical music or popular songs. Television was in its infancy; only some two million homes owned a set – and few people could receive a signal even if they wanted one. Most annual holidays were taken in Britain.

Attitudes, too, were very different. In general there was respect for authority, institutions and royalty, and those in the professions, such as doctors, lawyers, teachers and churchmen, still had an aura of infallibility. Many values and traditions which were soon to be challenged were still accepted without question. Even politicians were seen, almost by definition, as worthy of respect, and elections were fought on the doorstep and at well-attended rallies. Cabinet ministers were not expected to report to the media before addressing their parliamentary colleagues, and diplomacy was not conducted in public. Britain was not an intrusive society: 'In the public interest' was one thing; 'of interest to the public' was quite another and usually considered 'not cricket' – the accepted yardstick for honesty and decent behaviour.

These, though, were not unalterable attitudes: the changes in society, technology, medicine, communications and travel that were to transform life in the next 50 years were already beginning behind the scenes. Abroad, the former Empire was rapidly transforming itself into a Commonwealth of Nations, and Britain was developing new alliances elsewhere.

As an example of what was to come: in one decade (the seventies) Britain joined the EEC, went decimal, became an oil-producing nation, elected its first woman prime minister, watched Concorde go into service, survived a drought, endured soaring unemployment and a 'winter of discontent', and, almost inevitably, found the problems of Northern Ireland insoluble. There were four general elections and the country had four different prime ministers. It was not a quiet, stable period; nor was it unusual.

Early in 1952, however, the concerns of those in the United Kingdom and far beyond were for the new young Queen mourning the loss of her father, King George VI. That the monarchy in Britain would survive, flourish even, was hardly in doubt, and the mood of the people, once grief at the death of the King had diminished, was one of optimism. The war years were over, post-war austerity was beginning to ease, and the feeling was not merely that life could only get better, but that it would get better. Here was a new Elizabethan age, with a beautiful young Queen at the helm, and the Coronation was still to come!

1953 was indeed a memorable year: the Coronation itself and, right on cue for the Coronation, Everest was climbed for the first time, by a New Zealander and a Sherpa, both members of a British expedition; Stanley Matthews at last won an FA Cup Winner's medal; Gordon Richards at last won the Derby; and England, under the captaincy of Len Hutton, at last regained the Ashes from Australia.

Elsewhere in the world, Dwight Eisenhower was sworn in as President of the United States; Tito became President of Yugoslavia; King Hussein of Jordan and King Faisal II of Iraq were crowned; Nikita Khrushchev was elected First Secretary of the Soviet Union's Communist party; the Shah of Iran was restored to power; and, last but not least, the Korean war came to an end.

It was a world stage. The Queen, with Prince Philip at her side, was to travel constantly in the years to come, visiting, as head of state and head of the Commonwealth, parts of the world her predecessors had only heard of. Almost every possible mode of transport was used: car, train, plane, helicopter, boat and ship (particularly, of course, the royal yacht *Britannia*), state carriage, dugout canoe, the shoulders of South Sea islanders, elephant, and a golf buggy driven by President Tito. In this way, the face on the stamp, the official picture in the government office or school in, say, Barbados, materialised from time to time into a real person – though, 'Where is her crown?' was often heard when the Queen appeared in person.

For some 17 years these visits and tours remained pretty formal affairs. By the mid and late sixties they were clearly in need of a rethink, but it was not until the screening in 1969 of the trail-blazing, hugely popular documentary television film 'Royal Family' that real change came about. A year later the first of the royal walkabouts was introduced, in New Zealand, and after that crowds turning out for a royal visit knew they would see more than just a glimpse of the royal couple as they drove by; they would see them at first hand, close up, and might even have the chance to speak to the Queen or the Duke. When King George VI and Queen Elizabeth had moved among their people in the bombed towns and cities of Britain during the Second World War it had given similar pleasure, but the impact of the new approach in 1970 and afterwards was extraordinary.

The Queen was, however, not only a sovereign but also a wife and mother. She was in love with her handsome husband; Prince Charles and Princess Anne were

OPPOSITE *Balmoral in the summer of 1953: the Queen and Prince Charles help Princess Anne find a new way into the Castle.*

ABOVE *Every day, at home and abroad, the Queen has to deal with matters of state as well as with her personal correspondence.*

born before her accession, and two more boys were to follow later. It was at times hard to combine all these roles and the Queen Mother has played an important part when the Queen and Prince Philip were unavoidably absent. But 'the royal family' was, as the title of the 1969 documentary emphasised, the way in which the monarchy was to be projected for many years. It was an extended (and for a time a 'model') family in which the Queen's husband and later their children, but also her mother, sister and many other relatives, gave active and unstinting support, sharing official duties, representing her on occasions at home and abroad – all working diligently on behalf of 'the firm'. This concept of a model family, promoted so enthusiastically in the earlier years of the reign, was, however, to become something of an embarrassment.

It has been suggested that the end of Princess Margaret's marriage in 1976 marked the end of the role model royal family, but it was the younger members of the family who presented the media – and not only the British tabloids – with a supply of stories that editors like Kelvin McKenzie of *The Sun* could never have dreamed of.

The Princess Royal's separation and subsequent divorce from Mark Phillips, as well as her second marriage to a former equerry to the Queen, Commander Tim Laurence, were by and large free of rumour, innuendo and 'sleaze', and elicited public sympathy. More damaging were the breakdown and break-up of the marriages of the Prince and Princess of Wales and of the Duke and Duchess of York. When the second and third of their children's marriages also ended in divorce it was impossible not to feel sorry for the Queen and Prince Philip. They were determined to protect their grandchildren as much as possible from the adverse consequences of the break-ups, so Prince William and Prince Harry were as usual spending part of their long summer holiday with their father and grandparents at Balmoral when, early on Sunday morning, 1 September 1997, the news came through that Diana, Princess of Wales and her friend, Dodi Fayed, had been killed in a car crash while being driven through Paris.

Few people could have imagined the impact of the Princess's death on the people of Britain or the lasting effect on the monarchy itself. That extraordinary week had consequences far beyond the tragedy itself. If 1992 had been an annus horribilis, 1997 certainly led to a great deal of soul searching and reappraisal within Buckingham Palace. What was abundantly clear was that the British public had a very clear idea of the way they expected the royal family to function as the twentieth century drew to a close; it was also clear what they did not want. They did, for example, want a Union flag on Buckingham Palace to be flown at half-mast; they did not want to be told why, for archaic reasons of protocol, this could not be done. They did want some show of royal emotion; they did not want silence and a stiff upper lip. And the Queen took note.

However much the Queen is able to delegate to other members of her family, it is the monarch and only the monarch who can fulfill many of the duties (both constitutional and personal) of head of state. Even as a young woman (indeed, far younger than most of those with whom she worked) the Queen took her constitutional duties very seriously, as she does today. She reads her despatch boxes with intelligence and concentrated thoroughness, and with an ability to see the main thrust of the mass of detail in front of her. Early training in constitutional history gives her an awareness of the larger historical perspective and she is fascinated by world affairs, although, while remaining steadfastly apolitical, she also enjoys the minutiae of political life, the gossip. Like her mother, the Queen has a phenomenal memory.

In some respects, only the workload has changed over the years. For example, one of the Queen's more pleasant tasks is to send a telegram of congratulations to centenarians. In 1952 she sent about 300; by the end of the century almost 6,000; and it is estimated that by 2036 there will be 40,000 people of over 100 years in the United Kingdom. (Since the Queen herself would, by then, be 110, that last statistic is perhaps somewhat irrelevant, but it makes a point.)

When the Queen and the Prime Minister of the day are in London a weekly meeting is held on Tuesday evenings in Buckingham Palace (the time was changed when the Queen's children were little so that she and Prince Philip could join them at bathtime).

Prime ministers have valued these weekly audiences; the Queen's experience now covers 50 years, and the meeetings provide opportunities for discussion out of the public eye. Prime Ministers, however, are keenly aware that they must come thoroughly prepared, and Harold Wilson once confessed that he felt like a schoolboy who had not done his homework when the Queen mentioned a

ABOVE *A 'drive-about' during a tour of Australia in 1988. Something had obviously caught Prince Philip's attention.*

document which he himself had not read. The precise way in which the Queen advises and encourages her ministers will not be known for many years, but in his memoirs, *Time and Chance* (1987), James Callaghan notes how, early in 1976, the Queen encouraged him, as Foreign Secretary, to take an initiative, which he already had in mind, to resolve the Rhodesian problem: 'Inevitably the Queen's opinion was enough to tip the scales, for she is an authority on the Commonwealth and I respected her opinion.' The initiative failed but Callaghan commented, 'I had always thought since that the Queen's initiative on Rhodesia was a perfect illustration of how and when the Monarch could effectively intervene to advise and encourage her Ministers from her own wide experience and with complete constitutional propriety.'

When her first prime minister, Winston Churchill, retired in 1955, the Queen attended a farewell dinner at 10 Downing Street at which the old statesman spoke of 'the wise and kindly way of life of which Your Majesty is the young and gleaming champion'. (In later years the Queen revealed that she, too, had enjoyed her audiences with Churchill: 'It was always such fun.')

So many aspects of life in Britain – social, political, industrial, economic, academic, artistic, religious and sporting – have changed dramatically since the Queen's accession, but they have done so, Northern Ireland apart, virtually without bloodshed or extreme violence. In spite of the devolution of Scotland and Wales and the conflict in Northern Ireland, we are still, miraculously, a united Kingdom within the larger family of the Commonwealth.

When the Queen came to the throne in 1952, the multi-racial Commonwealth was in its infancy, containing only eight member states. None of the African or Caribbean states had achieved independence, and it was by no means certain that they would wish to maintain a relationship with the former colonial power when they did so. In the event, they all did, and today the Commonwealth has 54 member nations, all voluntarily choosing to cooperate over trade, aid, education, sport and, at times, defence or military peace-keeping operations. Of the 54, 16 (including the United Kingdom) are constitututional monarchies with the Queen as their head of state. Outside the United Kingdom she is represented by a Governor-General who, unless the Queen happens to be visiting that country, carries out all her duties. The Queen does go to each at regular intervals and for special anniversaries and celebrations.

This may change – indeed will change – and there has been some resentment in the Commonwealth as the United Kingdom has moved closer to Europe, but when, in 1999, the Australian referendum resulted in a 'no' to becoming a republic (or at least the kind of republic then on offer), most saw this as a strong personal endorsement of the Queen herself. Indeed, the Queen's ambition, as she said in her Christmas broadcast in New Zealand in 1953, has been 'to show that the Crown is not merely an abstract symbol of our unity but a personal and living bond between you and me'; and this she has achieved.

In its entry on the Queen, the *Royal Encyclopaedia* (1991) records her description of the Commonwealth as 'a voluntary association of equal partners in which no one claims pre-eminence'. In a speech to the Lord Mayor of London on 7 June 1977, in celebration of her Silver Jubilee, the Queen reflected that she had seen, 'from a unique position of advantage, the last great phase of the transformation of the Empire into Commonwealth and the transformation of the Crown from an emblem of dominion into a symbol of free and voluntary association. In all history, this has no precedent.'

The Queen is the first and only head the Commonwealth has had, and she sees it as a central part of her work to ensure that the links binding the member states within the Commonwealth are preserved and strengthened. (Prime ministers have sometimes disagreed.) In 1973 she attended the first Commonwealth Heads of Government conference to be held abroad (in Ottawa); since then she has attended all but one. She does not participate in the conference sessions but each president, prime minister or Commonwealth representative has the opportunity for a private meeting with her, and she presides at the traditional end-of-conference banquet.

The Queen has been fortunate not to have had to face the constitutional crises that so marked the reign of her grandfather, King George V. As early as 1910, in the first few months of the King's reign, Herbert Asquith carried through controversial measures to curb the power of the House of Lords. Thereafter, Home Rule for Ireland (still, at that time, united to the rest of Britain), the First World War (when the King's close cousins became enemies of Britain), the Russian Revolution (when the King was advised to repudiate requests from his Romanov cousins for safe haven from the Bolsheviks), the political instability of the post-war years, the General Strike of 1926 and the depression years all presented the King and his government with serious crises of a political and social nature.

Potential problems have nevertheless arisen for the Queen from time to time. During the 1970s the electoral success of the Scottish Nationalists made it seem possible that Scotland might separate itself entirely from the rest of the United Kingdom. The Queen alluded to this in Parliament on the occasion of her Silver Jubilee in May 1977, when she said, 'I number Kings and Queens among my ancestors and so I can readily understand these aspirations. But I cannot forget that I was crowned Queen of the United Kingdom of Great Britain and Northern Ireland. Perhaps this Jubilee is a time to remind ourselves of the benefits which union has conferred, at home and in our international dealings, on the inhabitants of all parts of this United Kingdom.' More recent moves in Scotland, Wales and Northern Ireland have, of course, brought the whole issue of the unity of the Kingdom very much to the fore again.

Constitutional problems and problems of sovereignty have also raised their heads in Commonwealth countries of which the Queen is head of state. In 1975 Sir John Kerr, Governor-General of Australia, in a striking exercise of his prerogative as representative of the Crown (though not, under the Australian constitution, directly of the Queen herself), dismissed the Prime Minister, Gough Whitlam, who had failed to get Parliament's approval for government expenditure. Since the Queen was never involved in this controversial episode, Buckingham

ABOVE *The Queen*
accepts flowers from
schoolgirls while
visiting the Australian
Centre for Christianity
and Culture in Canberra
in 2000.

Palace has never commented on it. Then, in 1983, the United States invaded Grenada, on the grounds that the uprising there might affect United States' security. The Queen, who is head of state of Grenada, was not consulted or informed (it is thought that the then American President, Ronald Reagan, had no idea of the Queen's position in the country), and Mrs Thatcher became 'incadescent'. In 1987, when Fiji suffered a military coup, declared itself a republic and left the Commonwealth, the Queen, in two open references to the event, stated first that anyone who sought to remove her representative in Fiji (the Governor-General) from office, 'would, in effect, be repudiating his allegiance and loyalty to the Queen', and, second, that she deplored the fact that 'the ending of Fijian allegiance to the Crown should have been brought about without the people of Fiji being given an opportunity to express their opinion on the proposal'. The status quo was eventually restored, though there was further unrest and rebellion in 2000.

The Queen's official engagements are arranged so that she can get to as many places and meet as many people as possible, both in the United Kingdom and overseas. After 50 years on the throne there are few towns and cities in Britain she has not visited, and she has stayed in all the Commonwealth countries. She now makes fewer overseas visits than in the past, but her energy and resilience still enable her to undertake at least two such taxing tours most years – either to Commonwealth countries, or state visits to foreign countries when ministers advise that a bit of that unique royal PR on behalf of the United Kingdom would not go amiss.

At home the Queen's annual programme is planned around certain fixed points. She is normally in London when Parliament is sitting (with weekends at Windsor Castle), but there are other annual fixtures: usually Sandringham for Christmas and the New Year; Windsor Castle at Easter and for Ascot week; a week at the Palace of Holyroodhouse in Edinburgh in July; and Balmoral Castle on Deeside for a late summer and autumn retreat from the limelight. There are other engagements which, for a variety of reasons, she is reluctant to miss: 'musts' in the domestic calendar include the Royal Maundy service on the Thursday before Easter Sunday (which takes place in a different cathedral each year); the Chelsea Flower Show at the end of May; the Royal Ascot race meeting following Trooping the Colour in mid June; and the Festival of Remembrance at the Royal Albert Hall and the Cenotaph ceremony on Remembrance Sunday in November. Add to these the 14 investitures held each year in the ballroom of Buckingham Palace, the three Palace garden parties, and state opening of Parliament (usually in November), and a considerable part of the annual official engagement jigsaw is already in place.

Other pieces are fitted in as the Private Secretary and other advisers sift through the invitations that come in, and make their recommendations as to which to accept. Overseas visits and tours (undertaken on Government advice unless entirely private) are normally fixed at least six months ahead.

When she is in London, the Queen's day might be spent entirely in the Palace, beginning, after breakfast with the newspapers, with official papers, personal correspondence and household business (menus, arrangements for visitors, staff

LEFT *The Queen and the Queen Mother chat to two of the owners at the North of Scotland Gun Dog Association Retriever Trials at Balmoral.*

news, for example), before the daily meeting with her Private Secretary. Briefings about those she would be seeing that day (an ingoing or outgoing ambassador, a newly appointed bishop, or a minister, for example) would prepare her for a series of audiences. Guests at one of the regular lunch parties might include an actor, a politician, a scientist, an author, someone from the world of sport, a trade union leader and an academic. After lunch, and a walk in the garden with the dogs, there would be more papers to read and digest, and possibly more audiences. Members of the royal household might also seek a few minutes of her time; if one was in need of advice, there was no better person to ask.

If there were no plans for the evening, the Queen would have a quiet, informal meal and there would be time to catch up with her mother and sister on the telephone, and perhaps watch television.

Another London day might begin in the same way but engagements could range from a formal visit to one of the professional bodies or institutions, to a

ABOVE *The 1994 Maundy Service was held in Truro Cathedral. As is the case each year, members of the Yeoman of the Guard were on duty.*

less formal one to a school or a hospital. An out-of-town programme could include a day or more in Wales or Scotland, or a visit to towns or regions that would enable the Queen to meet as wide a range of people as possible, or a visit to her armed forces. The trick of preparing these programmes is for the Private Secretary to plan as busy a day as time allows, yet leaving nobody feeling rushed.

The spread of television has meant that people everywhere can now see the Queen and members of the royal family without leaving home, but this has not stopped them turning out to see her in person when they can. Crowds in the cities and provincial towns of Britain are no smaller today than they were earlier in her reign. (This is partly because her visits are no longer civic dignitary in style – instead of just driving past as she did in the early days, she walks among the people, even protestors, stopping for a friendly word or to take a wilting bouquet from the warm and sticky hand of a small child.) Security is a worry, but on these occasions the Queen is seen at her most relaxed and natural. She tends to become stiff when talking directly to a television camera (indeed, when her Christmas message to the Commonwealth was first broadcast live on television in 1957 she admitted to finding it 'nerve-racking'). In the same way, the liveliness of her expression is often lost in a photograph.

The Queen is head of the armed services, and visits to regiments, ships and naval bases, and to the RAF are regularly included in her programmes. Whenever possible she also meets the families of serving men and women; during the Falkland war, for instance, she shared with other mothers and wives their concern for those involved in action.

However informal, a royal visit is by definition a special occasion, and the Queen is well aware that her arrival has been preceded by weeks of planning and preparation, and that this day is not like other days. Yet she does manage to meet an extremely diverse number of 'ordinary' people, and in a school children behave as children do, and in a hospital there is no hiding the experience of illness.

Immense attention to detail has always been paid in royal matters (meticulous records are kept of past programmes, for example) but today as much attention is given to the broader picture. Instead of the kind of ad hoc get-together that was held from time to time in the past to discuss, for instance, the education and early career of Prince Charles, a 'Way Ahead' group – a 'think tank' of family members and advisors – now meets regularly to look at future policy. The young Princes, William and Harry, are growing up in a family 'firm' that is far more businesslike and focussed than it has been for many decades – for many centuries, even; perhaps since a king last led his troops into battle!

This has brought about changes in the way things are done. Debutantes are no longer presented at court; guests at garden parties, private lunches, receptions and other events are now drawn from a far wider cross-section of the public; honours are now distributed to many more deserving recipients than used to be the case; royal expenditure is closely monitored and controlled; royal palaces and homes have been opened to the public; the royal collection is more accessible and works of art are often loaned to exhibitions. Jet planes, television and internet websites are all used to full advantage.

Within the royal household changes have also been made, aimed at bringing a greater professionalism and efficiency to the institution. Former civil servants, diplomats, businessmen and women – journalists even – have been appointed to the 'court', alongside the more traditional aristocrats and members of the Services. Those who now serve at Buckingham Palace work extremely hard but all in the royal household (the courtiers of today) have the sense of being involved in something totally worthwhile. The Queen does not 'demand' loyalty from her staff, she does not need to; it is given willingly and without reservation. She, in turn, is relaxed with and appreciative of those who work closely with her. Practical by nature, she concerns herself with the smooth running of the Palace, wanting to know in detail about appointments and departures, checking the dining-room before a banquet and going to have a look at the bedrooms before visitors arrive. She also knows the domestic and estate staff at her homes, and often their families too (those who live in the Royal Mews, for example, or on the farm at Windsor or the estate at Sandringham or Balmoral). Directly or indirectly through her senior staff, she will be aware of their problems and of good news.

For those members of the household who have also travelled on overseas tours and visits with the Queen, there is the additional pleasure of living for some of the time en famille, particularly when the royal yacht was in service. At these times the demands on someone who has to combine the roles of wife, mother, grandmother and conscientious head of state became very apparent. Stamina, patience, the ability to pay attention to detail and a prodigious memory are not the least of the Queen's qualities, but a sense of fun and an appreciation of the absurdities of life certainly help, too! There is, inevitably, the 'invisible barrier' between the Queen and those around her but she does have close friends.

As Press Secretary I was asked many personal questions about the Queen. Some were impossible to answer; one that I recall could, however, be answered easily: 'Does the Queen sweat?' We were in Australia and it was extremely hot. 'Doesn't seem to,' I replied. 'How come?' 'Well, just watch.' Sure enough, the Queen, who was watching a parade, stood almost stock still and unruffled while the rest of us fidgeted about, fanning ourselves, mopping our faces, doing everything in fact to make ourselves hotter than ever. The Queen knew this trick of the trade, as she does so many others. Cool indeed!

Once, as Michael Brunson, formerly of ITN, recalled in his autobiography, I was taken a mite by surprise. This time it was in the United States and advance copies of a speech the Queen was to make were being given out to the press. One American journalist wanted to know if she would stick to the script, or, as he put it, 'Is the Queen a textual deviant?' I was not the only one who needed a moment to make sure I had heard aright!

A much more predictable question that every Press Secretary has to deal with is, 'How much is the Queen worth?' (financially). Estimates are often wildly wrong, though no one would pretend that she is other than an extremely rich woman.

OPPOSITE *The Queen, Prince Philip and the Princess Royal leaving St George's Chapel, Windsor after a service in 1987.*

ABOVE *The Queen*
surrounded by her
family in 1998.

However, although she does personally own Balmoral Castle and Sandringham, the royal palaces, the royal collection, the art treasures and the Crown jewels are assets that are part of the national heritage, which belong to the Queen as sovereign and must be passed on to her successors.

Whatever her personal wealth, the Queen's hobbies and pleasures are essentially those of a well-off countrywoman. Most weekends of the year, certainly every August and September, every Easter and always in the New Year, the Queen and Prince Philip are in the country, regardless of Scottish or East Anglian weather. There are no lavish holidays in the world's sunspots, no nights at the casinos or in the clubs, no ostentation, no jet setting; instead she enjoys riding, long cross-country walks (hill-walking in the Highlands), attending race meetings, eventing or horse trials, walking the pack of corgis (which fight with those of the Queen Mother), picnicking with members of her family, doing crosswords and jigsaws, watching television, catching up on the latest films and books, and entertaining her guests in the country. More serious interests are horses and dogs. The Queen has an expert knowledge of both, and is a natural handler. She takes a practical interest in the breeding of her horses and is extremely knowledgeable about racing form. Her eye for horse flesh dates back to her childhood when she often advised her father, King George VI, on his horses.

Every single day of her life the Queen must attend to constitutional business but she knows exactly how she can best recharge her batteries and recognises how fortunate she is to be able to do so.

Throughout her reign the Queen has had the support, loyalty and love of her many immediate and close relatives – not least of her husband. Prince Philip's occasional gaffes and impatient outbursts have been outweighed a thousand times by his reassuring presence and support, his enthusiasm, his prodigious energy and the sharpness of his mind.

The role of consort is not an easy one. Queen Victoria's husband, Prince Albert, wrote feelingly: 'A very considerable section of the nation had never given itself the trouble to consider what really is the position of the husband of the Queen Regnant . . . [I was conceded] just as much space as I could stand on.' Prince Philip once exploded: 'I'm nothing but a bloody amoeba.' Yet he, like Prince Albert, has defined and developed his difficult role with imagination, integrity and wisdom. He has no official part in government affairs but, less constrained by protocol than the Queen, has been able to speak out, provoke discussion and take initiatives. Apart from his dedicated support of the Queen, he has a wide range of interests (the environment and conservation; science and technology; young people and sport; polo and, latterly, carriage driving) and his Duke of Edinburgh's Award Scheme has helped many young people reach a potential that might otherwise have been unfulfilled. He is a keen photographer and an accomplished painter, and takes seriously the overseeing of the farm at Windsor and the Sandringham and Balmoral estates.

Prince Philip is also closer to his children than has sometimes been assumed. Especially good with them when they were small, he tended to occasional impatience as they got older, and his expectations of the heir apparent have been difficult to live up to at times. But the Queen and Prince Philip's children (the 'fruit of their loins', as a Ghanaian radio commentator once described Prince Charles and Princess Anne) and grandchildren have provided the royal couple with all the joy, heartbreaks, happiness, frustrations, admiration, concerns, pride and anxiety experienced by most families.

The way in which the Queen and Prince Philip have brought up their children is a good indicator of the changes that have come about. Whereas the Queen and her sister were educated privately by a governess and tutors at home, all the young royals were sent to school (and to boarding school as they became older), and some went on to university. If they still lived in a way that most people in the country do not, they were at the very least growing up with their contemporaries. However, the children have always known that their ultimate loyalty – happily given – was to their mother. If their spouses found it difficult to adjust to royal life it is hardly surprising.

It has been an extraordinary five decades. From a window at the end of the Mall, as it were, the Queen has watched the transformation of Empire to British Commonwealth to Commonwealth; she has seen the frightening threat of the Communist bloc countries give way to the break-up of the Soviet Empire, symbolised by the demolition of the Berlin Wall and the reunification of Germany; she has marvelled as Nelson Mandela walked from prison to power, and rejoiced as the evil of apartheid was smashed in the polling booths rather than the battlefields; and almost every year since 1969 her Christmas message has included a plea and prayer for peace in Northern Ireland.

As aware of the privileges she enjoys as she is of her responsibilities, the Queen, with Prince Philip at her side, has served the country and the Commonwealth as a whole in splendid style for 50 years. An institution that could so easily have become an anachronism has, by evolving, retained a relevance and a purpose that is often the envy of others. Not many, perhaps, would today draw up a constitution based on a hereditary monarchy, but given the fact that the United Kingdom has a thousand years or more of such a system behind it, the maxim 'If it ain't bust, don't fix it' makes a very great deal of sense. Significantly (and this often seems to puzzle people in other countries), although the monarchy has been criticised, sniped at, satirised, and deemed irrelevant at times, and although we too have had our republican politicians and others with anti-monarchist agendas, there has not been an abolitionist or republican movement of any significance since the Queen ascended the throne. Whether this is due to the high esteem in which she herself is held or to the monarchy as an institution is not easy to determine, but there is no doubt about the personal regard and the very deep affection there is for the Queen. If ever destiny called on the right person to be in the right place at the right time it was in February 1952.

ABOVE *The corgis joined the Queen and Prince Philip when the photo was taken for the 1978 Christmas card.*

THE KING IS DEAD: LONG LIVE THE QUEEN

OPPOSITE King George VI saw his daughter for the last time on January 31 when she and the Duke of Edinburgh left London for a five-month tour of the Commonwealth.

The reign of Queen Elizabeth II began on February 6, not with the pageantry and rejoicing that was to mark the Coronation over a year later but with the nation and the former empire mourning the loss of King George VI. It was a sombre time, with the sympathy of millions going to the new Queen, to her mother, Queen Elizabeth, and to her sister, Princess Margaret. There were special thoughts also for the new Queen's grandmother, Queen Mary, widow of King George V, who had already experienced the death of two of her five sons.

The Queen's accession took place under particularly poignant circumstances which endeared her further to people throughout the world. She and Lieutenant Philip Mountbatten, newly created Duke of Edinburgh, had been married in Westminster Abbey on 21 November 1947, a wedding which had lightened the gloom of post-war austerity. Prince Charles had been born almost exactly a year later, and his sister, Princess Anne, in August 1950. King George VI and Queen Elizabeth delighted in the experience of being grandparents but a cloud hung over the royal family – the health of the King. The war years had taken their toll; so too had years of smoking.

In July 1951 the Duke of Edinburgh was given indefinite leave from the Royal Navy – a career that he loved – in order that he could support his wife as she took on more of her father's responsibilities. In late summer the King's left lung was removed, following the discovery of a malignant growth. The operation was a success and in October the Princess and the Duke felt able to leave for five weeks on an official visit to Canada and the United States.

The King appeared to continue to make a good recovery and a day of National Thanksgiving was held in December. Nevertheless, it was felt that it would be unwise for the King to go ahead with a planned tour to East Africa, Australia and

LEFT *On February 6 special editions of the evening papers brought Londoners the news of the King's death overnight at Sandringham.*

New Zealand in the new year; instead, on 31 January 1952, the Princess and the Duke again left London to carry out the visit on his behalf. The King insisted on going to the airport to see them off, and indeed on standing on the tarmac waving farewell until the aircraft was out of sight. Six days later, in the early hours of February 6 King George VI suffered a coronary thrombosis and died peacefully in his sleep at Sandringham, his home in Norfolk.

At the time of his death the new Queen was at the Aberdare Forest Game Reserve in Kenya, where she had been photographing the wildlife from an observation post at the Treetops Hotel. Prince Philip, told of the King's death as the couple were preparing to go on to Mombasa, broke the news to his wife. When Martin Charteris, the Princess's Private Secretary (later to become the Queen's Private Secretary), saw the new Queen shortly afterwards, needing to discuss the many arrangements that had to be made, he asked her by what name she would wish to be known. (Her father had taken the name George on his own accession, although he had been christened Albert and was always known in the family as Bertie.) 'Why, Elizabeth of course,' was the response. 'Her grief was immense,' Charteris recalled later, 'her sense of duty equally so.'

The Queen and the Duke flew home as soon as transport could be arranged. As the Queen came down the steps of the BOAC Argonaut at Heathrow she looked poised, assured, yet, at barely twenty-five, vulnerable. Waiting hatless in the bitter cold on the runway to greet their new monarch were the Prime Minister, Winston Churchill, with other senior politicians and officials. Each, it seemed, was old enough to be her father.

Immediately ahead of the Queen lay onerous tasks. Even as she mourned the loss of a deeply loved father, affairs of state had to be attended to. Her life was about to be transformed: to the roles of wife and mother were now added those of

We belong, all of us, to the British Commonwealth and Empire, that immense union of nations, with their homes set in all the four corners of the earth. Like our own families, it can be a great power for good – a force which I believe can be of immeasurable benefit to all humanity. My father and my grandfather before him worked all their lives to unite our peoples ever more closely, and to maintain its ideals which were so near to their hearts. I shall strive to carry on their work.

Extract from The Queen's Christmas Message

sovereign and head of state – or simply, to the world, the role of Queen.

The day after her return to London she was formally proclaimed Queen and attended an Accession Council. To her Declaration of Sovereignty, she added a promise, saying without faltering, 'My heart is too full to say more to you today than that I shall always work as my father did.' The next days of mourning were shared by millions of her subjects. A third of a million mourners, after queuing for many hours, filed past the catafalque where the King lay in state in Westminster Hall. Members of the royal family paid their own private tributes and messages of condolence poured in from leaders around the world.

The funeral of King George VI was held at Windsor on February 15 and slowly the country began to adjust to what was already being labelled 'the new Elizabethan age'.

In April the Queen approved a proclamation declaring 'her will and pleasure that she and her children shall be styled and known as the House and Family of Windsor and that her descendants who marry and their descendants shall bear the name of Windsor'. Windsor, the name coined by King George V, was to remain the dynastic name.

The Queen and her family moved from Clarence House to Buckingham Palace, and her mother and sister took over Clarence House – which has remained the Queen Mother's home to this day. It was a difficult period of adjustment for the Queen Mother, and for Princess Margaret who in the recent years had come to enjoy almost more public attention than her elder sister. A new pattern of life was soon established at the Palace – a pattern inevitably different from what had gone before though the understanding and appreciation of the monarch's role remained unchanged. This was the rock, together with an unshakeable Christian faith, which provided the foundation for the new Elizabethan reign.

1953

THE CROWNING MOMENT

KEY EVENTS

Josef Stalin died in March, leaving the Soviet Union's hierarchy to fight a war of succession.

• • •

President Tito took control in Yugoslavia.

• • •

Dag Hammerskjöld became the United Nation's secretary-general.

• • •

The Korean war ended in July but British troops found themselves involved with the Mau Mau uprising in Kenya.

• • •

The Federation of Rhodesia and Nyasaland was formed.

• • •

Floods on the east coast of England caused nearly 300 deaths and immense damage to property.

• • •

Winston Churchill won the Nobel Prize for literature.

• • •

The Welsh poet Dylan Thomas died.

• • •

On the eve of Coronation Day came the news of the conquest of Mount Everest by Edmund Hillary of New Zealand and Sherpa Tensing of Nepal, members of the British expedition led by Col John Hunt.

OPPOSITE *The crowning moment. The Archbishop of Canterbury raises the St Edward's crown before placing it on the Queen's head.*

RIGHT *For the millions in London on Coronation Day every moment of the long wait was worthwhile.*

$\mathcal{C}$oronation Day, Tuesday 2 June 1953, is one of those events of which people say, 'I remember exactly where I was and what I was doing.' Such occasions are all too often associated with tragedy (the assassination of President Kennedy; the death of Diana, Princess of Wales) but that happy June day is remembered for the enthusiasm of the crowds (despite the rain), for the processions of carriages and mounted cavalry, for the music inside the Abbey and the bands outside, and for the service itself. But it is remembered above all else for the beauty, the poise, the sincerity and the happiness of the young Queen, accompanied and supported by her husband. For 50 years the Duke of Edinburgh has somehow managed to be an ever-present consort while at the same time remaining his own man. On Coronation Day, on what of all days was the Queen's day, he was an obvious source of love and strength to the sovereign.

The Queen, with the Duke of Edinburgh at her side, was driven from Buckingham Palace to Westminster Abbey in a gold coach pulled by eight grey horses. Commonwealth and other world leaders had preceded them in carriages, and a memorable sight was that of the immense Queen Salote of Tonga beaming and waving as her open carriage filled with rainwater.

In the Abbey, in the presence of royalty of many countries, of presidents, prime ministers, peers and commoners, the Queen took the Coronation Oath in a

clear, strong voice. The actual moment of crowning came when the Archbishop of Canterbury held high the St Edward's crown before placing it reverently on the sovereign's head. Then the great shout went up: 'God Save the Queen!'

The only sad note for the Queen was that her grandmother, Queen Mary, had not lived to see her crowned. She had died on March 24.

Back at Buckingham Palace the Queen and the Duke made six appearances on the balcony to greet the cheering crowds, alone or with their children or with other members of the royal family. They last came out onto the balcony at midnight and it was only with the greatest reluctance that the crowds which had stretched right down the Mall and all around the Palace eventually began to disperse.

At the insistence of the Queen herself (her Prime Minister, Winston Churchill, disapproved), the Coronation was shown on BBC television and was watched, worldwide, by millions. In Britain many people rented sets for the first time in order to watch the event, and it confirmed the role that television was to play in our lives. The Queen still broadcast her Christmas message on radio; it was not until 1957 that she broadcast live on television. At the end of the Coronation year her theme was her devotion to the Commonwealth and its ideals.

So, with feelings of optimism, goodwill, affection and, indeed, love, the post-Coronation reign of the second Elizabeth got under way. The Queen was to travel constantly in the years to come, visiting, as head of state and head of the Commonwealth, parts of the world her predecessors had only heard of or had to read about, but the six-month tour of the Commonwealth on which the Queen and the Duke embarked in November 1953 was the longest they were to make. The SS *Gothic* was used as a floating Palace while the royal yacht *Britannia*, which the Queen had launched in April, was being completed in time to bring the royal party home on the last leg of the tour from Gibraltar to London.

Some people have expressed the hope that my reign may mark a new Elizabethan age. Frankly, I do not myself feel at all like my great Tudor forbear, who was blessed with neither husband nor children, who ruled as a despot and was never able to leave her native shores.

Extract from The Queen's Christmas Message

The Queen's couturier, Norman Hartnell, with his designs for the Queen's coronation dress. Hartnell designed clothes for Queen Mary, and was later responsible for the 'look' associated with the Queen Mother. He designed many of the exquisitely embroidered and highly decorated state and evening dresses worn by the Queen, and continued to work for her until shortly before his death in 1979. Thereafter, Sir Hardy Amies became the most significant influence on the Queen's clothes, making many of her softly tailored suits. Ian Thomas, trained by Hartnell, and John Anderson have since made many of her outfits.

1954

NATO voted to end the occupation of West Germany and to form a Western European Union.

•••

The European convention on Human Rights came into force.

•••

The Mau Mau uprising in Kenya by now involved many British troops, mostly national servicemen.

•••

Gamal Abdel Nasser became the head of state in Egypt. Britain agreed to withdraw its garrison troops from the Canal zone subject to guarantees of free passage through the canal.

•••

A BOAC de Havilland Comet crashed in the Mediterranean, resulting in 35 deaths and the grounding of all Comets in service.

•••

Rationing in Britain finally ended in July, nine years after the end of the Second World War.

•••

Myxomatosis all but wiped out Britain's rabbit population.

•••

Roger Bannister ran the first sub-four-minute mile.

DOWN UNDER AND BEYOND

*T*he hugely successful tour of the Commonwealth on which the Queen and the Duke of Edinburgh had embarked in the previous November finally ended at Gibraltar on May 11. The newly commissioned royal yacht *Britannia* had brought Prince Charles and Princess Anne to meet their parents, and they were to sail with them as they returned to London. The children had been in the charge of their grandmother, the Queen Mother, during their parents' absence. For the royal family this was not only a happy family reunion but the beginning of a love affair with *Britannia* which was to last for well over 40 years.

The tour itself had been a triumphant success, had broken much new ground and had set the pattern of other foreign tours that would follow in the years to come.

Since arriving in Bermuda in November 1953, the Queen had travelled 43,618 miles, attracting enormous crowds wherever she landed. Jamaica had been the second port of call, and from there *Gothic* had sailed through the Panama Canal, where there was a brief, formal stop, and on to the South Pacific. It was the first visit by a reigning monarch to Fiji, Tonga, New Zealand and Australia; Edward VIII had visited the countries as Prince of Wales. The programmes arranged for the Queen and the Duke allowed for little informality compared with

LEFT *The Queen and the Duke of Edinburgh board HMAS* Australia *at sea off Townsville, Queensland, during their tour of Australia. On the left is Captain A.W.R. McNicoll, commander of the ship's company.*

OPPOSITE *In Malta, the Queen and Countess Edwina Mountbatten, with Prince Charles and Princess Anne, arrive at the Marsa Ground to watch their husbands play polo.*

subsequent tours, but the enthusiasm of the people more than made up for this.

After calling at the Cocos Islands, spending ten days in Sri Lanka (at that time still called Ceylon) and a day in Aden in the South Yemen, *Gothic* took the royal couple on to Malta and finally Gibraltar. En route, the Queen and the Duke also spent two days in Uganda.

For the Queen, the tour brought home as nothing else could have done the significance of her role as queen of so many diverse territories and peoples, and the advantages to these countries of belonging to the Commonwealth. The wisdom that so many Commonwealth leaders were to appreciate in later years was based on information and observation gathered, assimilated and stored during the tour. In the same way, many of the principles she had already come to value as princess were reinforced and were to remain throughout her reign.

For the last stage of the journey – on *Britannia* – the Queen was also joined by her Prime Minister, Winston Churchill. During a television documentary programme in 1986 the Queen recalled that as they were coming up the Thames to London, where she – ever practical – saw 'dirty, muddy, brown water', Churchill talked of the river as 'the silver thread running through the heart of the kingdom'.

The Commonwealth tour was fully covered by BBC radio and by cinema newsreels but meanwhile television had been rapidly extending its reach and impact. There were indications of the colossal changes that this new form of communication was to bring about, and the Pope, Pius XII, warned of its dangers. Certainly, royal advisors were alert to the impact it was to have on the popular perception and understanding of the monarchy.

The Queen remained in the country for the rest of the year, and received two state visits: the King and Queen of Sweden came to London in June, and Emperor Haile Selassie of Ethiopia in October.

ABOVE *From the moment of the Queen's return to Britain, the Prime Minister, Winston Churchill, had been a close and valued adviser to the whole royal family.*

RIGHT *Emperor Haile Selassie of Ethiopia was welcomed to London by the Queen in October. His was only the second incoming state visit of the Queen's reign (the first visitor had been the King of Sweden), and it marked the close relations between Britain and Ethiopia at that time.*

1955

The Eastern bloc countries signed the Warsaw Pact to counteract the West's alliances.
West Germany joined NATO.

•••

Juan Perón resigned as President of Argentina and left the country.

•••

Violence in Cyprus, Algeria and Vietnam involved British and French forces. In Cyprus a state of emergency was declared, as a result of EOKA terrorism.

•••

Immigrants from the West Indies started to arrive in Britain. Many found work on the railways and buses, and in the National Health Service.

•••

Plans to electrify the railways and to start work on a network of motorways throughout Britain were announced by the Government.

•••

Commercial television was introduced to Britain when ITV went on air in September.

•••

The physicist Albert Einstein died in America. His Theory of Special Relativity was one of the cornerstones of modern physics.

RIGHT *The Queen and Prince Philip are escorted to their car by Sir Winston Churchill after attending a dinner at 10 Downing Street to mark the Prime Minister's retirement.*

CHURCHILL FINALLY STEPS DOWN

*T*he Queen exercised two prerogatives for the first time: she accepted the resignation of a prime minister and appointed a new one.

For men and women of all political persuasions, the resignation in April of Sir Winston Churchill as Prime Minister marked the end of an era. Churchill and King George VI had led Britain through the war years, and although defeated in the 1945 elections Churchill had returned to lead the country again; now, at eighty, he was handing over the reins to Sir Anthony Eden. Churchill had been the Queen's first prime minister and the two had immediately formed bonds of respect and affection that were to prove of immense value to both. Eden was her first appointment.

Churchill was in ill health but, choosing to stay on in his beloved House of Commons as a backbencher, he turned down the dukedom offered to him by the Queen.

Meantime, Princess Margaret had serious decisions of her own to make. She and Group Captain Peter Townsend, a former equerry to King George VI and equerry to the Queen, were known to be in love but he had been divorced and the prevailing view was that they could marry only if the Princess gave up her right to

LEFT *The nation's memorial to King George VI is unveiled by the Queen in Carlton Gardens just off the Mall in London. The work of William Macmillan, the statue shows the King in naval uniform.*

OPPOSITE *The Queen with camera poised at the Olympic Horse Trials at Badminton. Princess Margaret and, standing behind her, Captain Peter Townsend, watch the cross-country event.*

the accession. In October Princess Margaret announced that she had decided to end the relationship: 'Mindful of the Church's teaching that marriage is indissoluble and conscious of my duty to the Commonwealth I have resolved to put these considerations above all others.'

The Princess was with the Queen and others of the royal family when a statue of King George VI was unveiled just off the Mall. A portrait of the Queen, by the Italian artist Pietro Annigoni, was shown in the Royal Academy summer exhibition and attracted huge crowds.

A hundred years ago our knowledge of the world's surface was by no means complete; today most of the blanks have been filled in. Our new explorations are into new territories of scientific knowledge and into the unknown regions of human behaviour. We have still to solve the problem of living peaceably together as peoples and as nations.

Extract from The Queen's Christmas Message

The winning captain is congratulated by his wife as the Queen makes the presentations after polo at Windsor Great Park. Prince Philip played regularly until a wrist injury forced him to give up the sport. He then moved on to competitive four-in-hand carriage driving.

Prince Philip's uncle, Lord Mountbatten, was also an enthusiast and, with their encouragement, Prince Charles became an accomplished and regular player.

SUEZ DIVIDES BRITAIN

*B*oth domestically and internationally 1956 proved to be a post-war watershed. It was a strange but significant time. Many post-war realities were finally brought home to the United Kingdom and the Queen found herself involved in events which divided the country.

Early in the year the Queen and the Duke of Edinburgh spent three weeks in Nigeria. In the north of the African continent, General Abdel Nasser took full executive power in Egypt, a move which was to have far-reaching consequences.

When President Nasser nationalised the Suez Canal in July the British Government, in what came to be regarded as collusion with France and to some extent Israel, effectively declared war on Egypt. At the beginning of August the Queen was attending the racing at Goodwood when she received a message from the Prime Minister, Anthony Eden, asking her to sign a proclamation ordering 20,000 army reservists to be called up for service in the Canal zone. She gave her approval at Goodwood and signed the document later that day at a special Privy Council meeting at nearby Arundel Castle.

After bombing raids on Port Said and other targets, an Anglo-French force of paratroops landed in Port Said but the Anglo-British action did not have the support of the Americans, and there was much opposition at home. By the beginning of November the United Nations had forced a ceasefire and a UN force moved into the Canal zone. The Queen had acted entirely constitutionally throughout the Suez crisis, while not necessarily supporting Eden's policy, but Britain was never again able to act in such an outmoded imperialistic way. Lady Eden later said that at times she had felt as though the Suez Canal was flowing through the sitting room of 10 Downing Street, and Suez was indeed to prove too much for her husband's fragile health.

LEFT *The Daily Mirror seemed uncertain but the other papers had no doubt – the Suez crisis had escalated into war. Britain attacked Egypt on October 31.*

OPPOSITE *The Queen and Prince Philip spent nearly three weeks in Nigeria early in the year. The programme included a Durbar at Kadona and many meetings with tribal leaders.*

Meanwhile, hopes had been raised worldwide of better relations between East and West. In January the Soviet leader Nikita Khrushchev had denounced Josef Stalin in an astonishing attack on his predecessor, and in April Khrushchev and Marshal Bulganin came to Britain on an official visit. While taking tea with the Queen and Prince Philip at Windsor Castle, they presented the Queen with a thoroughbred horse as a 30th-birthday gift. However, later in the year, old-fashioned imperialism – Soviet-style – again reared its head when Khrushchev sent Soviet tanks into Hungary to quell the anti-Communist rising there.

RIGHT *The leaders of the Soviet Union, Nikita Krushchev and Marshal Bulganin, arrive in London for an official visit designed to improve Anglo-Soviet relations.*

LEFT *The Duke of Edinburgh began a five-month tour of the Commonwealth in October, giving the scandalmongers and gossip columnists an unwarranted field day.*

On the domestic front another matter was to concern the Queen and the Duke of Edinburgh. In mid October the Duke left for a five-month world tour, prompting gossip about such a long absence from his wife and children. It was not helped when, towards the end of the tour, the Duke's Private Secretary, Michael Parker, who was with him, was sued for divorce on the grounds of adultery. The Duke was seen to suffer guilt by association and imaginations went into overdrive, resulting in an official denial from Buckingham Palace: 'It is quite untrue that there is any rift between the Queen and the Duke of Edinburgh' was the wording of the statement issued by the Queen's Press Secretary, Commander Richard Colville RN.

At home the Queen Mother suffered a disappointment when her horse, Devon Loch, ridden by Dick Francis (later to become a best-selling author), stumbled when leading in the run-in at the end of the Grand National and was beaten by ESB.

If my husband cannot be at home on Christmas Day, I could not wish for a better reason than he should be travelling in other parts of the Commonwealth.

Extract from The Queen's Christmas Message

1957

THE CHRISTMAS MESSAGE ON TELEVISION

*T*he Queen began a new tradition when for the first time her Christmas
message to the Commonwealth was broadcast from Sandringham not only on
radio but live on television. Well over 16 million viewers tuned in at 3 pm, among
them the rest of the royal family in an adjoining room. The Queen found it 'nerve-
racking'.

Earlier in the year the Queen had appointed the third prime minister of her
reign when Sir Anthony Eden resigned for reasons of health and was succeeded by
Harold Macmillan. Suez had proved too much for Eden. His replacement could
well have been R.A. Butler, but the Queen acted on the advice of the Conservative
party's hierarchy.

The Queen made another appointment, in February, when the Duke of
Edinburgh returned from his world tour. She accorded him the style and title of
Prince of the United Kingdom in acknowledgement of his services to the country
of his adoption and to the Commonwealth, 'culminating in the tour which has just
concluded'. Here was a formal end to the rift that never was, and a new title for
the Queen's husband: HRH The Prince Philip, Duke of Edinburgh.

RIGHT *Formal
informality perhaps
best describes the
charming Christmas
card the Queen and
Prince Philip sent to
their friends in 1957.*

It has always been easy to hate and destroy.
To build and to cherish is much more difficult.
That is why we can take a pride in the new
Commonwealth we are building.

Extract from The Queen's Christmas Message

ABOVE *The Queen may have found her first live televised Christmas message from Sandringham 'nervewracking', but there was no hint of strain when she was photographed immediately after the broadcast.*

ABOVE *The Queen
addressed the General
Assembly of the
United Nations when
she and Prince Philip
visited the UN
Headquarters in
New York in October.
The UN Secretary-
General, Dag
Hammarskjöld, is
seated above left.*

The royal family, however, came in for some unexpected criticism when the *National and English Review* published a wide-ranging critique of the monarchy by its editor, Lord Altrincham (the historian and biographer John Grigg). By current standards it might not seem remarkable but at the time great was the wrath that descended on the noble lord. Much of this anger was caused by Lord Altrincham's criticism of the Queen's speeches, both in content and delivery, but not everyone (including some in the Palace), thought he was too wide of the mark. Indeed, some years later Sir Martin Charteris told John Grigg (he had by then renounced his title), 'You did a great service to the monarchy.' Malcolm Muggeridge's contribution to the debate was perhaps less well received when he coined the phrase 'the royal soap opera'. Like Lord Altrincham he was, for a while, banned from broadcasting by the BBC.

However, the royal family remained popular, there was no real advantage to be gained from pointing out its failings, and the hubbub soon died down.

Later that year the Queen and Prince Philip paid a state visit to the United States where the President (who was in his second term of office) and Mrs Eisenhower welcomed them to the White House. In New York, the Queen addressed a special meeting of the United Nations' General Assembly.

1958

KEY EVENTS

Charles de Gaulle was elected President in France, and Nikita Khrushchev took supreme control of the Soviet Union.

• • •

King Faisal of Iraq was murdered and a republic proclaimed.

• • •

The de Havilland Comet went into transatlantic service with BOAC.

• • •

The Campaign for Nuclear Disarmament (CND) was formed in Britain.

• • •

September saw race riots in Notting Hill in London.

• • •

Mike Hawthorn became the first British World Motor Champion.

• • •

Returning from a European Cup game in Belgrade, the plane carrying the Manchester United team, several club officials and the press corps, crashed while attempting to take off from Munich. Seven of the team and eight journalists were killed, and many more were injured.

RIGHT *A sign of the times and of reconciliation. The Chancellor of the German Federal Republic, Konrad Adenauer, was entertained by the Queen at Buckingham Palace.*

CHARLES TO BE PRINCE OF WALES

A rare occurrence – illness (an operation on her sinuses) – prevented the Queen from carrying out some of her engagements during 1958. She was unable in person to announce that she intended to create Prince Charles Prince of Wales; instead, her tape-recorded message was played at Cardiff Arms Park during the closing ceremony of the Commonwealth Games. The news was enthusiastically received. Prince Charles was still only nine years old, and his investiture would eventually take place in 1969.

Prince Charles was by now boarding at Cheam School near Newbury, which

RIGHT *The Queen inaugurated the country's direct-dialling telephone system when she made a trunk call to the Lord Provost of Edinburgh from the Bristol telephone exchange.*

his father and other members of the family had attended. The Queen had been educated privately at home but she and Prince Philip were determined that their children should have as 'normal' an education as possible and that Prince Charles should 'go to school with other boys of his generation and learn to live with other children'. For a sensitive child brought up in the Palace it was a hard lesson.

The Queen was now into the seventh year of her reign and although the essential style of the monarchy was little altered, changes like this were gradually being introduced. This year, for example, debutantes were presented at Buckingham Palace for the last time – in its way a significant development. The list of guests invited to garden parties at Buckingham Palace was also being drawn from more walks of life.

In March the Queen and Prince Philip were in the Netherlands as guests of Queen Juliana and Prince Bernhard. And for the first time since the end of the Second World War the heads of state of Italy and of the German Federal Republic came to Britain: President Gronchi in May, and President Heuss in October.

On the domestic front, the Queen inaugurated the national telephone system's direct dialling with a phone call from Bristol to Edinburgh. However, the Buckingham Palace switchboard was still manually operated at the time, so when the Queen phoned her mother, Queen Elizabeth – or vice versa – the operator would say, 'Your Majesty, Her Majesty, Your Majesty'.

It's a good time to remember those around us who are far from home, feeling perhaps strange and lonely. My own thoughts are with the men and women and children from other parts of the Commonwealth who have come to live and work in the great cities of this country and may well be missing the warmth and sunshine of their homelands.

Extract from The Queen's Christmas Message

1959

A SECRET WELL KEPT

KEY EVENTS

The Prime Minister, Harold Macmillan, made 'a voyage of discovery' to the Soviet Union and then went on to meet US President Eisenhower in the White House.

• • •

Singapore became a self-governing state with a new constitution.

• • •

Fidel Castro seized power in Cuba; the Dalai Lama fled from Tibet to India as the Communist Chinese overran his country; and Mrs Indira Gandhi was elected President of the ruling Congress party in India.

• • •

Motorists could now buy the BMC Mini, designed by Alec Issigonis.

• • •

The Manchester Guardian went national as The Guardian newspaper.

• • •

The British film actor Errol Flynn died, as did the painter Sir Stanley Spencer. The racing driver Mike Hawthorn was killed in a car crash – not on the circuit but on the Guildford bypass in Surrey.

The six weeks that the Queen and Prince Philip spent in North America in June and July took them to many parts of Canada. Much of the country's population, apart from those of French descent who were mainly in Quebec, had British ancestry, and the welcome was warm – as it was when the royal couple crossed the border into the United States to spend a day in Chicago.

One of the highlights of the tour was the moment when the Queen and President Eisenhower jointly opened the St Lawrence Seaway, connecting the Atlantic to the Great Lakes and forming one of the most important seaways of the world.

Throughout the tour the Queen kept secret the fact that she was expecting her third child early in 1960. It was announced on August 7 to general delight; nearly ten years after the birth of Princess Anne, the Queen and Prince Philip were starting a second family

In September President Eisenhower came to Britain and spent some time as

RIGHT *The Queen and President Eisenhower after they had together opened the great new St Lawrence Seaway.*

LEFT *A picture that could have been taken on any day the Queen was in Britain. Ever present, the 'boxes', the paperwork, the friend!*

BELOW *A very special relationship continued as President Eisenhower spent time with the royal family at Balmoral Castle.*

guest of the Queen and Prince Philip at Balmoral. There was no doubt about the liking the Queen and the President had for each other; it dated back of course to the war years and the friendship between Ike and King George VI. The two heads of state became regular correspondents.

As the fifties ended, the Queen could look back with a good deal of satisfaction on the (nearly) eight years of her reign, although there was much to concern her, too, in the dispatches from Cyprus and Kenya, from the Indian subcontinent and beyond. It was not a peaceful world. There would be international problems ahead, and it was clear that life in the United Kingdom would change greatly in the years ahead.

1960

A Birth, a Wedding and a Sixtieth

KEY EVENTS

An American U2 spy plane was shot down over the Soviet Union and the pilot, Gary Powers, imprisoned by the Russians for 10 years for espionage.

• • •

On a visit to Cape Town Prime Minister Harold Macmillan spoke of 'wind of change'. A month later the South African police killed 56 black Africans at Sharpeville.

• • •

Somalia, Ghana and Cyprus became independent republics; Nigeria gained independence and President Makarios became the first President of the new Republic of Cyprus.

• • •

The Israeli intelligence service, Mossad, arrested Adolf Eichmann in Argentina for atrocities committed against Jews during the war.

• • •

In Britain, national service came to an end.

• • •

Aneurin Bevan, Health Minister when the National Health Service was introduced in 1948, died in July.

• • •

Francis Chichester sailed the Atlantic for the first time single-handed in Gypsy Moth II.

The sixties began with three major events for the royal family: Prince Andrew was born at Buckingham Palace on February 19; Princess Margaret announced her engagement to the photographer Antony (Tony) Armstrong-Jones and was married in Westminster Abbey on May 6; and on August 4 Queen Elizabeth, the Queen Mother celebrated her 60th birthday.

The Queen's new son became second in line of succession, taking precedence over his sister Anne. The engagement of Princess Margaret to a working commoner, albeit with a double-barrelled name and one of the country's leading photographers, was warmly welcomed. There was a general feeling that after the 'Townsend affair' the Princess deserved all the happiness she could get and that the lack of a title was an irrelevance. Buckingham Palace, however, thought differently, and a year after his marriage Tony was created Earl of Snowdon, thus ensuring that any children of the marriage would, as grandchildren of a sovereign, have a title. On her marriage, though, the bride became HRH The Princess Margaret, Mrs Antony Armstrong-Jones.

August 4 was the Queen Mother's 60th birthday and 'Happy birthday, ma'am' was heard from just about everyone. Some wag commented at the time that

RIGHT *Prince Andrew has an early photo-call, sharing the limelight with his sister and father.*

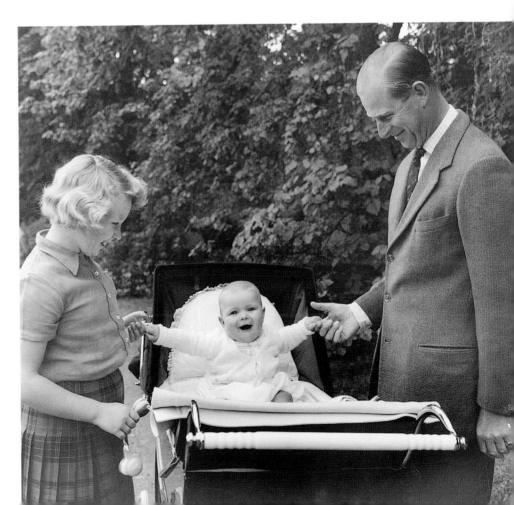

although she was the same age as the century, the Queen Mother was in much better shape!

Prince Philip and other members of the Mountbatten family had been disappointed when the Queen, at the beginning of her reign, had confirmed the family name of Windsor. Now she amended this: descendants who did not bear the title HRH, and females who might marry, would from now on carry the name Mountbatten-Windsor.

President de Gaulle paid a state visit to Britain in April, staying as guest of the Queen in Buckingham Palace. This was a highly sensitive occasion, and all appeared to go well. It did not, however, result in the President coming round to the view that Britain was ready to join the Common Market. 'Non!' was still the reaction.

The Queen also received visits from the King and Queen of Thailand and the King and Queen of Nepal. Unusually, she made no overseas visits herself this year; the baby Prince probably had something to do with that.

Civilisation as we know it, or would like it to be, depends upon a constant striving towards better things. In times of stress, such as we are living through, only a determined effort by men and women of goodwill everywhere can halt and reverse a growing tendency towards violence and disintegration.

Extract from The Queen's Christmas Message

A SHOOT IN INDIA; A DANCE IN GHANA

For the Queen and Prince Philip 1961 was one of the busiest years, with nine major overseas visits included in the twelve-month programme. First, in January, they left a wintry London for a six-week tour of India and Pakistan and a state visit to Nepal. Visits to the Indian subcontinent (whether by members of the royal family or by an English cricket team) often have their problems, and on this occasion Prince Philip provoked the wrath of animal welfare groups and endangered species organisations by shooting a tigress. Apart from this the visit went well, with the Queen clearly impressed by the progress in both countries since partition and independence.

There were predictable protests, too, from some sections of the Protestant churches when the Queen had a private audience with Pope John XXIII during her first state visit to Italy and the Vatican City in May.

ABOVE *The Queen meets Pope John XXIII in the Vatican.*

OPPOSITE *The splendid pageantry of a state occasion in India. It is hot in the sub-continent in January!*

ABOVE *The 'trophy' – a tigress; the marksman – Prince Philip. Controversial even at the time, there would be no such shoot ever again.*

LEFT *The Queen with India's first Prime Minister, Jawarlal Nehru. He fought for independence but kept India in the Commonwealth.*

Earlier, the Queen and Prince Philip had been in Iran as guests of the Shah; later they went to Liberia, Sierra Leone and to Ghana, the last of these visits postponed from 1960 when the Queen's pregnancy was announced. By 1961 the Ghanaian leader, Kwame Nkrumah, was already running what was virtually a one-party state, and there were those in Westminster and Whitehall who would have preferred the visit to be further postponed. Macmillan was desperately concerned about the Queen's safety, but also about the diplomatic repercussions of a second cancellation. In the end he advised the Queen to go, which was what the head of the Commonwealth had had every intention of doing.

In the event the tour proved hard work but valuable. In the unlikely setting of Accra the Queen was able to speak of the Commonwealth as a family in which it was perfectly possible to have disagreements and to discuss them. Some people in South Africa (by now no longer a member of the Commonwealth) were outraged by press photographs of the Queen dancing with the Ghanaian President; the Ghanaian press was delighted!

Finally, after Ghana and Sierra Leone, the Queen and Prince Philip went on to The Gambia, where the British had once prospered as a result of the slave trade.

At home, the Queen visited Glasgow where she spent time in the Gorbals and had an enthusiastic reception.

Hats worn by the Queen are designed, not only to be attractive, but also to suit the occasion and to allow the Queen's face to be seen. Simone Mirman, a Frenchwoman, the Australian Frederick Fox, Philip Somerville and Patey Ltd are among those who have regularly designed for the Queen – tiaras apart!

1962

THE PRINCE OF WALES AT SCHOOL IN SCOTLAND

The Queen and her sister had been educated at home by a governess, Crawfie, who taught them the basics. Constitutional history, the study of genealogy, music and French had been provided by additional tutors as the Queen grew older.

Unlike his mother, who in her early years had not been expected to inherit the throne, Prince Charles's destiny had always been clear; his entire life has, in a sense, been a preparation for becoming sovereign. The Queen and Prince Philip had clear ideas about the education they wanted for their children, and felt it important that Prince Charles should mix with other children. Prince Philip had been one of the first pupils at Gordonstoun School, near Elgin in Scotland, so it

RIGHT *The 11-year-old Prince Charles started his first term at Gordonstoun School on May 1. His father, a former pupil, showed him round.*

ABOVE *The Queen with the Commonwealth heads of government in the White Drawing Room at Buckingham Palace in September.*

was no surprise when, in May, the 13-year-old Prince was taken by his father to the school. Founded by the German progressive educationalist Dr Kurt Hahn in 1934, it was a school that had a reputation for cold showers and toughness but in fact aimed at an all-round education to develop the whole child. Pupils were encouraged to explore their own abilities. The two younger Princes were also to go to Gordonstoun, and seem to have enjoyed it rather more than their older brother.

The Queen made no overseas tours in 1962, but President Tubman of Liberia and King Olav V of Norway paid state visits to Britain. It was in other parts of the world, however, that headlines were being made.

The Cuban missile crisis dominated world affairs, when East and West seemed to come as close to nuclear war as was possible without the button actually being pressed. The Soviet Union, it was confirmed beyond doubt, was shipping missiles to Cuba, which constituted a direct threat to the United States. President Kennedy, rejecting the possibility of a direct attack on Cuba, opted instead to blockade the Soviet ships, giving a clear threat that military action would be taken if the blockade were breached.

For a while all-out war seemed more than probable – a

Mankind continues to achieve wonders in technical and space research, but in the western world perhaps the launching of Telstar has captured the imagination most vividly. This tiny satellite has become the invisible focus of a million eyes. Telstar, and her sister satellites as they arise, can now show the world to the world just as it is in its daily life. What a wonderfully exciting prospect and perhaps it will make us stop and think about what sort of picture we are presenting to each other.

Extract from The Queen's Christmas Message

war which would inevitably have involved Britain in support of her allies – but in the end Khrushchev called back his convoys and the missiles already in position were dismantled. Throughout the crisis Harold Macmillan made sure the Queen was fully briefed and consulted.

The early part of the year saw more changes within the Commonwealth: in the Caribbean, the West Indian Federation was dissolved and Trinidad, Tobago and Jamaica became independent, as, in Africa, did Uganda. All chose to remain within the Commonwealth.

A former American secretary of state, Dean Acheson, upset many with a speech suggesting that Britain was 'played out' and was now a country without a role. The Queen was certainly among those who were concerned that the country's role vis-à-vis Europe on the one hand and the Commonwealth on the other should be clarified and expressed positively. More than one Commonwealth leader took the opportunity to express his views to the Queen during the Commonwealth Heads of Government meeting in London in September, but that the United Kingdom did have a role was not questioned.

DEATH OF THE PRESIDENT

KEY EVENTS

The American President, J.F. Kennedy, was assassinated in Dallas on November 22.

• • •

Britain, the USSR and the United States signed a nuclear test-ban treaty.

• • •

President de Gaulle of France vetoed British entry into the EEC.

• • •

Kenya and Nigeria became Commonwealth republics. Malaysia became a new nation.

• • •

At a rally in America black civil rights leader Martin Luther King described his dream of a united America.

• • •

In Britain, John Profumo, Secretary of State for war, resigned after lying to the House of Commons in denying an affair with a call-girl, Christine Keeler, who was also the mistress of a Russian naval attaché.

• • •

Mailbags with contents worth £2½ million were stolen when the Glasgow to London mail train was held up on August 8.

For the Queen, like so many others, 1963 was a turbulent, tragic year.

The beginning of the year saw John F. Kennedy President of the United States, Harold Macmillan Britain's Prime Minister, Hugh Gaitskell leader of the Labour party and a lesser figure, John Profumo, Secretary of State for war. The British Government was planning to enter the European Common Market and a gang of London-based criminals was planning to rob a mail train.

By the end of the year President Kennedy had been assassinated; Macmillan had resigned; Gaitskell had died; Profumo was disgraced; and President de Gaulle had again blocked British membership of the Common Market with a resounding 'Non!' Only the train robbery seemed to have gone according to plan.

In October the Queen became involved in the aftermath of Harold Macmillan's resignation. The Conservative party – in conference in Blackpool at the time – was left in turmoil. It was only after a puzzling process of consultations (elections for the leadership of the Conservative party had not yet been introduced) that the Queen, advised by Macmillan whom she visited in hospital, invited the then Lord Home to become Prime Minister. If he was no one's first choice, he seemed to be everyone's second. In order to take a seat in the House of Commons he had to renounce his peerage (becoming Sir Alec Douglas-Home) and fight a by-election.

Earlier in the year, the Queen and Prince Philip had toured New Zealand and Australia, calling at Fiji en route. They received an affectionate welcome but enthusiasm was tempered as a result of Britain's European aspirations. There was

OPPOSITE *A Maori chief meets the Queen at Waitangi, New Zealand. She had earlier addressed 7,000 Maoris, wishing them, in their own language, 'Good health to you all!'*

RIGHT *Prince Philip, representing the Queen (with Prime Minister Sir Alec Douglas-Home on his right), joins the mourners in Washington DC, following the requiem mass for President John F. Kennedy.*

Six holders of the Victoria
Cross, all from the Royal
Welsh Regiment, were
presented to the Queen when
she visited the Welsh Brigade
Depot. As Head of the Armed
Forces the Queen ensures that
contact with all three services
and with those who served
their country in earlier years is
a regular part of her annual
programme. As well as visiting
service establishments, she is
kept fully briefed by
government ministers. There
is, of course, a strong naval
tradition in the royal family.

fear that the economic links of the past would be severed, and that patriotic and
sentimental ties could be weakened. There was also some resentment that these
were the first visits by the Queen for nearly ten years to countries of which she was
head of state.

There was much controversy about a state visit to Britain by King Paul and
Queen Frederika of Greece in July. The visit was punctuated by demonstrations
against the Greek government whose civil right's record was particularly criticised,
and against Queen Frederika, a German princess by birth, who had been involved
in the Hitler Youth Movement and was perceived as a right-wing influence on
Greek affairs. There was booing when the two royal couples went to the theatre in
London's West End, and Harold Wilson, the Labour leader, declined an invitation
to the state banquet as an expression of his party's disapproval of the visit.

Despite the horrors and disappointments of the year the public were delighted
when it was announced, just before Princess Anne started the next stage of her
schooling at Benenden, that the Queen was again pregnant.

1964

BIRTH OF EDWARD

The end of a remarkable political career ended on July 27 when Winston Spencer Churchill MP entered the chamber of the House of Commons for the last time. He had first done so before the First World War, and had gone on to lead the coalition National Government that saw Britain through the ravages of the Second World War. He had been the Queen's Prime Minister for the first three years of her reign.

Churchill's departure from the political scene anticipated by only a few months the end of 13 years in power for the Conservative party. In the October general election Sir Alec Douglas-Home's Conservatives were beaten by Harold Wilson's Labour party. If Home, the Scottish aristocrat, was the prime minister

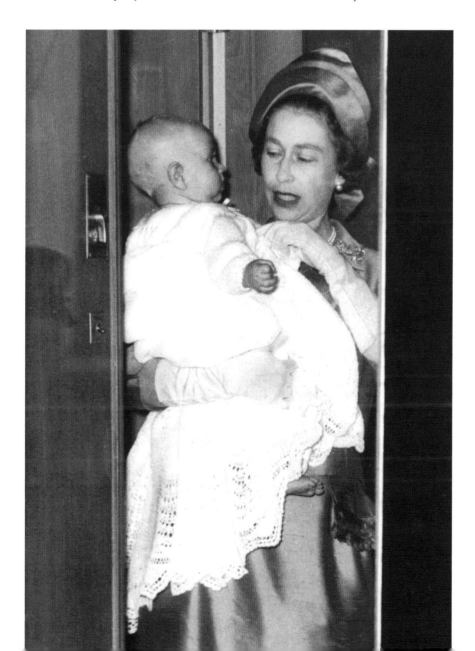

RIGHT *The three-month-old Prince Edward in safe hands as the royal train leaves London for Balmoral.*

who had most in common with his monarch in terms of background, the Yorkshire 'technocrat' had the least. Despite this, the Queen and her new Prime Minister quickly established a relationship which Wilson came to appreciate greatly. Over the next 12 years, with one break, Wilson was to lead three different Labour administrations.

When Harold Wilson was called to Buckingham Palace and asked to form an administration, the Queen's third son, Edward, was eight months old. Born on March 10, he had been just three months old when the Queen had carried her new son on to the balcony of the Palace after the annual Trooping the Colour ceremony. By October, when she and Prince Philip spent nine days in Canada, the

ABOVE *The Queen and Prince Philip's two youngest children, Prince Andrew and Prince Edward, with their parents on the balcony of Buckingham Palace after the annual Trooping the Colour parade.*

RIGHT *Prince Edward is the centre of attention on the Queen's Christmas card.*

BELOW *The Queen at the State Opening of the Canadian Parliament in Ottawa in October. Visits to her Commonwealth monarchies are often timed so that she may open the new Parliamentary session in person.*

Some speak today as though the age of adventure and initiative is past. On the contrary, never have the challenges been greater or more urgent. The fight against poverty, malnutrition and ignorance is harder than ever, and we must do all in our power to see that science is directed towards solving these problems.

Extract from The Queen's Christmas Message

Queen was fully 'back in business'. The tour was expected to have its difficult days and this proved to be the case in Quebec where the French-speaking separatists demonstrated against the monarchy and the Canadian police over-reacted. It left the Canadian Prime Minister, Lester Pearson, who had initiated the visit, somewhat embarrassed.

At home President Abbod of the Sudan was welcomed on a state visit – an indication of Britain's continuing interest in what was formerly the Anglo-Egyptian Sudan.

1965

GREAT LEADERS REMEMBERED

*W*inston Churchill died on January 24. The old warrior, journalist, politician, statesman, author, historian and painter was 90. The Queen broke with royal tradition by attending the state funeral, held in St Paul's Cathedral six days later, and leading the nation in its mourning.

Almost immediately after the funeral the Queen and Prince Philip left to pay state visits to Ethiopia and the Sudan.

In May, on the site at Runnymede where King John signed the Magna Carta in 1215, the Queen dedicated an acre of wood and grassland to the memory of the late President Kennedy. Mrs Kennedy and her children, Caroline and John, listened as the Queen gave the land to the American people 'in memory of a man whom in death my people still mourn and whom in life they loved and admired'. A simple memorial of Portland stone commemorates the President's life. For much of the ceremony young John Kennedy clasped Prince Philip's hand.

Later in the year the Queen found herself involved in the confrontations between Harold Wilson and the Prime Minister of Rhodesia, Ian Smith, who was insisting that a white minority government should continue to rule. Wilson was urging democratic elections for the country, on the 'one man, one vote' principle. Both invoked the Queen's support in an attempt to solve the Rhodesian crisis but

OPPOSITE *The Queen, who led the nation's mourning for Sir Winston Churchill, leaves St Paul's Cathedral with other members of the royal family at the conclusion of the funeral service.*

RIGHT *Jacqueline Kennedy, her children John and Caroline and their uncle Robert Kennedy, are greeted by the Queen before the unveiling of the John F. Kennedy memorial at Runnymede.*

despite receiving a letter from the Queen expressing hope for a negotiated settlement (which Smith was to cite as support for his actions) the Smith government declared UDI (Unilateral Declaration of Independence) in November, and the regime was declared illegal.

Other royal engagements included a state visit to West Germany, now officially named the German Federal Republic. The programme took the royal visitors to Berlin, where they visited the Berlin Wall dividing the city.

Towards the end of the year a decision about the further education of the Prince of Wales needed to be made. A meeting was held at the Palace in December, which included, among others, the Queen, Earl Mountbatten of Burma, the Prime Minister, the Archbishop of Canterbury and the Chairman of the University Vice Chancellors' Committee. It was agreed that the Prince should go to Trinity College,

BELOW *The horror of the Berlin Wall is brought home to the Queen and Prince Philip during their visit to the then divided city in May.*

OPPOSITE *The Duke and Duchess of Windsor leave Westminster Abbey after attending a memorial service for the Princess Royal, the Duke's sister and aunt of the Queen and Princess Margaret.*

Cambridge, and then to the Britannia Royal Naval College at Dartmouth before, following his father's example, embarking on a career in the Royal Navy.

The country as a whole continued to enjoy the sixties, the young relishing new freedoms of expression, of rebellion, of travel and of dress, making it clear that there was a real and deep 'generation gap'. The royal family might still be behaving much as usual, though even the royal hem lines went up, but for many other families life seemed very different from that of even a decade earlier.

'Peace on earth' – we may not have it at the moment, we may never have it completely, but we will certainly achieve nothing unless we go on trying to remove the causes of conflict between people and nations.

Extract from The Queen's Christmas Message

The Queen and her corgis provide one of the enduring personal images of the reign. The first royal corgi was bought by her father, the then Duke of York (later King George VI) in 1933 when the Queen was seven. She has been devoted to the breed ever since, and looks after her own dogs as much as possible; they travel with her from house to house, where they live in her private apartments. When one dies it is buried in the grounds of whichever residence is being used at the time. Three of the longest-living – Susan, Sugar and Heather – have gravestones at Sandringham. On occasions, one of the Queen's corgis has mated with a dachshund belonging to Princess Margaret, resulting in the birth of the royal 'dorgis'.

1966

TRIUMPH AND TRAGEDY

KEY EVENTS

Mrs Indira Gandhi became Prime Minister of India. Kwame Nkrumah, President of Ghana, was overthrown.

•••

Dr Hendrik Verwoerd, the South African Prime Minister, was stabbed to death by a white extremist.

•••

In China, Chairman Mao unleashed his cultural revolution and published his Little Red Book.

•••

British statisticians estimated that there were a million new 'Commonwealth and Pakistan' residents in the country.

*T*he general election of 1966 confirmed Harold Wilson's Labour government in power, with an overall majority of 96. The State Opening of Parliament by the Queen, which followed, was televised for the first time, and the ancient ritual drew a substantial audience. Later, in July, a Welsh Nationalist MP, Gwynfor Evans, took his seat in the House of Commons for the first time.

On July 30 the Queen was at Wembley Stadium to watch the final of the 1966 World Cup and present the Jules Rimet trophy to the England captain, Bobby Moore. The entire nation – with the possible exception of the Scots and the Welsh – shared her pleasure and delight.

October 27 was a very different occasion. The Queen was in the small mining village of Aberfan in Wales to weep with the people there. Together they mourned the 146 – mostly children – who had died six days earlier when a slag heap collapsed and hundreds of thousands of tonnes of mine waste, rocks, sludge and mud slid down to engulf the Pantglas Infants and Junior School. That day, without reservation, the entire nation joined the Queen in sharing the grief of those in Aberfan.

The disaster left Britain numb. The pictures from the scene were terrible,

RIGHT *The triumph at Wembley. The World Cup is England's, safely in the hands of the captain, Bobby Moore.*

ABOVE *The tragedy at Aberfan. The Queen and Prince Philip share in the heartbreak and grief.*

In the modern world the opportunities for women to give something of value to the human family are greater than ever, because, through their own efforts, they are now beginning to play their full part in public life.

Extract from The Queen's Christmas Message

moving even the most experienced and hardened to tears – so much so that many of the images shot that day were never shown. Prince Philip and the Prime Minister had gone immediately to Aberfan but the Queen had waited, feeling that her presence might have distracted from the rescue work.

When the Queen and Prince Philip paid a visit to Northern Ireland in July the 'troubles' were still three years away, though the situation was ominously simmering below the surface. There was considerable alarm, however, when the car in which they were travelling was hit by a concrete block dropped from a building along the route. Luckily, neither the Queen nor Prince Philip was hurt. In the south, Eamon de Valera, though by now 83, was elected President of the Irish Republic for a second seven-year term. Jack Lynch became Prime Minister later in the year.

The Queen and Prince Philip had spent February in the Caribbean. Later in the year they paid a visit to Belgium. Guests at Buckingham Palace included President Jonas of Austria and King Hussein of Jordan and his then wife, Princess Muna.

BELOW *The Queen, at the British Aircraft Corporation works at Filton, Bristol, is shown a model of Concorde.*

1967

KEY EVENTS

During the Six-Day war the Israelis defeated the combined forces of Egypt, Jordan and Syria, transforming the situation in the Middle East.

•••

President de Gaulle again vetoed British entry to the EEC.

•••

Uganda became a republic. South Yemen declared a Peoples' Republic.

•••

In Britain, BBC2 began television transmissions in colour. The pound was devalued in November.

•••

A giant oil tanker, the Torrey Canyon, *ran aground between the Scilly Isles and Land's End causing devastation to wildlife.*

•••

The former Labour Prime Minister Clement Attlee died. So too did the former West German Chancellor Konrad Adenauer.

•••

The American actress Jayne Mansfield was killed in a car crash and Donald Campbell, attempting to beat his own world water speed record of 276 mph, was killed when Bluebird somersaulted on Coniston Water at a speed approaching 300 mph.

RIGHT *The QEII slips dramatically into the River Clyde after being named and launched by the Queen.*

ARISE SIR FRANCIS – AGAIN!

*A*lmost 400 years after Queen Elizabeth I had knighted Francis Drake at Greenwich following his circumnavigation of the world in the *Golden Hind* in 1580, Queen Elizabeth II used the same sword on the same spot to bestow a knighthood on another Francis: Francis Chichester who was, at the age of 65, the first man to sail round the world single-handed. A splendid public ceremony at Greenwich rounded off the epic voyage of the new Sir Francis.

Still at sea, as it were, the Queen launched the liner *QEII* at Clydebank in September, while one of the ship's illustrious predecessors, the great three-funnelled liner *Queen Mary*, sailed from Southampton on her final voyage – to Long Beach, California.

Another special and very personal royal occasion took place in London in June. A plaque commemorating the life of Queen Mary, who had died in March 1953, was unveiled by the Queen in memory of her grandmother. The Duke and Duchess of Windsor both came to the ceremony and were greeted warmly by both the Queen and the Queen Mother. It was the first time the Duchess had been to any royal gathering since her husband had abdicated.

LEFT *Francis Chichester is knighted by the Queen at the Royal Naval College, Greenwich.*

Before taking their summer break at Balmoral the Queen and Prince Philip spent some time in Canada, visiting Expo 67 in Montreal and joining in the Canadian centennial celebrations. The welcome they received was warm enough but in Quebec there was more enthusiasm shown when President de Gaulle paid a visit and, playing to the separatist gallery, he raised hopes by saying France would support moves for French-Canadian independence. Nevertheless, the Queen remained, firmly, '*la Reine du Canada*'.

The Queen was deeply upset when she heard that her Australian Prime Minister, Harold Holt, had been drowned. The messages of condolence she immediately sent to his family were reinforced when Prince Charles flew to Australia to represent the Queen at the funeral service.

RIGHT *The unveiling of a statue of Queen Mary brought together all the senior members of the royal family, including her sons, the Dukes of Gloucester and Windsor, and their wives.*

BELOW *Prince Charles arrives at Trinity College, Cambridge, at the start of his first term, to read, initially, archaeology and anthropology.*

King Faisal of Saudi Arabia and President Sunay of Turkey paid state visits to Britain.

Meanwhile, discussions were taking place about a possible television documentary programme on the monarchy. This would film the royal family in the Palace, and at the other royal homes: Windsor, Sandringham and Balmoral.

Let there be no doubt that Britain is faced with formidable problems, but let there also be no doubt she will overcome them. Determined and well directed effort by a people who for centuries have given ample evidence of their resources of character and initiative must bring its reward.

Extract from *The Queen's Christmas Message*

ASSASSINATIONS, RIOTS AND A DOCUMENTARY

*A*part from state visits to Brazil and to Chile, this comparatively quiet year for the Queen was spent mainly in the United Kingdom. Her family were growing up. Prince Charles, now up at Cambridge University, was 20 in November, and with his sister and brothers was enthusiastically involved in the filming of the BBC/ITV consortium's documentary, 'Royal Family'. He was also concerned with the preparations for his investiture as Prince of Wales, which was to take place the following July at Caernarfon Castle.

Of considerable significance to the royal household and to the public perception of the monarchy was the retirement after 20 years of Commander Richard Colville RN from his post as press secretary to the Queen. Colville was definitely of the 'old school' and had a positive dislike of the press with whom he had to work.

His successor and former assistant, William Heseltine, was an Australian with experience of a world beyond the armed services and the Palace – the proverbial breath of fresh air. While appreciating the Queen's demarcation lines about what was public and what was not, he was nevertheless able to introduce a much more relaxed and therefore more positive style into Palace–press relations. Without his

RIGHT *During an eight-day visit to Chile the Queen found herself guarded by mini cavalry mounted on decorated tricycles when she visited a school, the Escuela Inglaterra.*

ABOVE *In Salvador,*
Brazil, the Queen's car
stopped for a young
ballet student to
present a bouquet to
the royal visitors.

understanding and drive the landmark television documentary 'Royal Family'
would not have been as successful as it proved to be. The Queen, of course, had
the last word but, encouraged by Prince Philip and advised by Heseltine and the
film producer Lord Brabourne, she agreed that the time was right for the
monarchy to embrace television. The documentary, when it was shown around the
world, proved hugely popular.

The South American visits were a great success. President da Costa e Silva was
the royal couple's host in Brazil; in Chile it was President Frei, whose term in office
was soon to end with the election of the left-wing leader Salvador Allende.

A Prince for Wales; Royals Head for the Red

The documentary that gave unprecedented access to the private life of the Queen and her family, 'Royal Family', had its television première in June, and was seen by 40 million viewers in the United Kingdom and many more around the world. An immediate success, it left an inquisitive public begging for more.

In very different ways two princes had their destinies confirmed in July. The Queen invested her son Charles Prince of Wales at an investiture in Caernarfon Castle, in a ceremony largely designed by Lord Snowdon in his capacity as Constable of the Castle. Millions watched on television throughout the world. The same month, General Franco, the Spanish Fascist dictator, proclaimed Prince Juan Carlos his heir and future King of Spain.

Events in Northern Ireland were very different from the pageantry in Wales. Violence had broken out in Londonderry in January, and a civil rights march in Belfast ended in mayhem. The Roman Catholic community was demanding 'one man, one vote'. Major James Chichester-Clark, who had succeeded Terence O'Neill as Prime Minister of Northern Ireland in May, requested the presence of British troops to guard key installations. At the time, British ministers hoped that this would be a 'limited operation', with law and order soon restored. It was an unrealistic hope; the 'troubles' had well and truly – and tragically – begun.

In October the Queen welcomed Emperor Hirohito of Japan on a state visit to Britain. Coming only 24 years after the end of the Second World War, his visit provoked protests from former prisoners-of-war and a chillingly cool response from the public. More welcome were President Saragat of Italy and President Urho Kekkonen of Finland. The Queen, accompanied by the Duke, visited Austria.

LEFT *Not your everyday commuter. The Queen travels on the London Underground after inaugurating the Victoria Line service.*

OPPOSITE *The crowning moment as the Queen invests Charles as Prince of Wales in the grounds of Caernarfon Castle.*

During the year the Queen became the focus of criticism in the press when *The Times* reported that she was overspending her Civil List allowance. Prince Philip caused a major stir on American television when, asked on NBC's 'Meet the Press' if the royals could no longer balance their budget, he confirmed that the royal household had indeed overspent its allowance: 'We go into the red next year. Now inevitably, if nothing happens, we may have to – I don't know – move into smaller premises.' 'Nothing', it transpired, did not happen. For the first time in the Queen's reign a debate began over the cost of the monarchy and whether it gave value for money. As a result of this, an all-party committee of MPs was set up to assess the situation, and duly reported in 1971.

On the world stage the Queen was joined by new names and new faces: Golda Meir became Prime Minister of Israel; a young army officer, Muammar Gaddafi, took power in Libya, overthrowing King Idris; and Yasser Arafat became leader of the Palestine Liberation Organisation (PLO). All were to become significant players and (in the case of the last two) remarkable survivors.

1970

A 'Cook's Tour' – and Royal Walkabout

KEY EVENTS

In Rhodesia, Ian Smith declared a republic.

•••

Fiji gained its independence.

•••

Canada declared a state of insurrection in Quebec.

•••

Princess Margaret and Lord Snowdon travelled to Yugoslavia to stay with President Tito.

•••

In Northern Ireland, the British Army fired rubber bullets at protestors in Belfast for the first time. The Revd Ian Paisley, Minister of the Free Presbyterian Church in Northern Ireland and leader of the Democratic Unionist Party, won a by-election and took his seat at Westminster.

•••

In London, race riots overshadowed the Notting Hill Carnival.

*T*he new decade began as the old one had ended – with political unrest, violence in Northern Ireland, and industrial, economic and social problems at home. Vietnam, South Africa and the Middle East continued to dominate the headlines with war, apartheid and hijackings.

At the start of the year, the Queen and Prince Philip set off, in February, on an eight-week tour to Fiji, Tonga, New Zealand and Australia. 'Cook's Tour', as it became known, marked the 200th anniversary of James Cook's landings in different parts of Australasia. Some three months after the royal visit, Fiji and Tonga declared their independence, and Prince William of Gloucester travelled to Tonga to represent the Queen at their independence celebrations. The Commonwealth now had just 12 members.

While the Queen was away, it became increasingly clear that a general election would be called – in which 18-year-olds would have the vote for the first time (they had been able to vote in a by-election in Bridgwater in March). Prime Minister Harold Wilson called the election for June 18 and the Conservatives won with an overall majority of 31.

On her return, the Queen accepted Harold Wilson's resignation and asked Edward Heath to form a new administration. Edward Heath (politician, sailor, musician) was to remain at 10 Downing Street for three years; it was to prove a difficult time for the Government and for the country.

The Queen's two eldest children increasingly played a more public role. Early in the year it was announced that, after completing his studies at Cambridge, Prince Charles would take a short flying course at RAF Cranwell before following the family tradition and joining the Royal Navy. He and his sister, Princess Anne,

RIGHT *In October Edward Heath entertained the Queen and President Nixon at Chequers, the Prime Minister's official country residence.*

OPPOSITE *At Sandringham,
Prince Charles points out
details of a model of
Captain Cook's ship
Endeavour to his parents
and to his sister, Princess
Anne, before the royal tour
to Australasia.*

accompanied the Queen and Prince Philip on their tour of Canada in June, to join the centennial celebrations in the Northwest Territories and Manitoba. Charles and Anne then travelled to Washington, where they were guests of President and Richard Nixon. The Queen was invited to Chequers by Edward Heath in October when he gave a lunch in honour of President Nixon. Elsewhere in the world, the key figures in many countries were being replaced: in Egypt Anwar Sadat became President following the death of Gamal Abdel Nasser; in France Charles de Gaulle died just a year after ending his second spell as President; Chile had a new President in Salvador Allende; in Portugal the Fascist dictator António Salazar died in July; and in Syria General Hafez el-Assad took power.

The Queen observed these changes, sending messages of condolence or congratulations as appropriate. Her own workload continued to increase, but she also found time to relax. In November, at the National Portrait Gallery in London, she unveiled the second portrait to be painted of her by Pietro Annigoni.

The Queen, like her mother, is an expert judge of horses. During the year she attended several race meetings (the 'sport of kings'), and several of her horses won. On the flat Nijinsky won the Two Thousand Guineas and the St Leger, as well as triumphing in the Derby at Epsom. Later in the year the Queen granted a royal charter to the Jockey Club, the first governing body of any sport to be awarded such an honour. The racing world was sad when Arkle – that most appealing of steeplechasers – had to be put down.

'The strength of the Commonwealth lies in its history and the way people feel about it. All those years through which we have lived together have given us an exchange of people and ideas which ensures that there is a continuing concern for each other.'

Extract from The Queen's Christmas Message

The Queen is an enthusiastic and competent horsewoman, although she is often criticised for riding without a helmet. At Windsor, as here, or at Balmoral and Sandringham, she takes every opportunity to ride out and to chat to friends and families working on the estates. The Queen's love of exercise – walking as well as riding – and of the outdoors undoubtedly contributes to her consistent and continuing good health.

1971

KEY EVENTS

President Pompidou of France declared the way clear for Britain to join the EEC.

• • •

Delegates from mainland China took their seats at the United Nations for the first time.

• • •

Tito was re-elected President of Yugoslavia.

• • •

In Uganda, Idi Amin seized power, expelled all Ugandan Asians, and had thousands of his opponents murdered.

• • •

The first British soldier was killed in Northern Ireland since peace-keeping troops were sent in in 1969. Riots followed the introduction of internment and there were bomb attacks on mainland Britain.

• • •

At Ibrox Park in Glasgow, a safety barrier collapsed during the Rangers–Celtic match on New Year's Day: 66 spectators died.

• • •

The Haitian dictator Papa Doc Duvalier, the former Soviet leader Nikita Khrushchev, the Soviet composer Igor Stravinsky and the American jazz trumpeter Louis Armstrong died.

THE CIVIL LIST REVIEWED

*W*ith the co-operation of all departments in Buckingham Palace an all-party committee of MPs, including the royal family's most outspoken critic, Willie Hamilton MP, was formed to review the Civil List – the money voted by Parliament to maintain the royal household, and support the Queen as head of state and some other members of the royal family in carrying out their public roles. (The Prince of Wales's income comes from the Duchy of Cornwall.)

The Civil List had stood at £475,000 a year since the Queen's accession in 1952, nearly 20 years earlier. The committee now recommended, in view of inflation, that this should be increased to £980,000 a year, with extra monies for certain members of the family. There would be no allowance for the Queen's personal use.

The recommendations were eventually approved, though by no means unanimously. Forty-three MPs voted against, among them the former leader of the Liberal party, Jo Grimond.

The Queen, Prince Philip and Princess Anne went to Canada (to British Columbia this time) and to Turkey, where a state of emergency was suspended for the duration of the visit! Imposed because of political unrest in the country, this would, apart from anything else, have prevented crowds gathering. In the event an enthusiastic welcome awaited the royals on a visit that took in Gallipoli and Ephesus as well as Istanbul and Ankara.

Mrs Gandhi, Prime Minister of India, President Tito of Yugoslavia and the Kings of Norway and Afghanistan all visited the Queen this year. So, more controversially, did Emperor Hirohito of Japan. As a result of Japan's conduct in the Second World War, particularly the treatment of prisoners-of-war, there was strong opposition to the visit. His public reception was cool, and the Queen, speaking at the state banquet in Buckingham Palace, said that such terrible things must not be allowed to happen again. In his speech, Hirohito made no mention of the war whatsoever.

A census taken on April 25 revealed that there were 55,346,551 men, women and children living in the United Kingdom that day – over two and a half million more than in 1961. Despite this, fewer were living in London and the other big urban centres, though more than ever seemed to have to travel to them to go to work. What all 55 million had to get used to was decimal coinage. D-Day, as it had become known, was February 15 but the Decimal Currency Board had for months been preparing the nation for life without shillings. From now on we would only be able to deal in pounds and pence – a hundred of the latter to one of the former, and although theoretically much easier to deal with not to everyone's taste.

LEFT *The Queen is given a helping hand as she hops ashore from a floating platform on a visit to Turkey.*

ABOVE *The Queen greets Emperor Hirohito of Japan at London's Victoria Station as he arrives for a controversial state visit.*

A KING IS MOURNED

KEY EVENTS

The world was horrified when 11 Israeli athletes in Munich for the Olympic Games were murdered by Arab terrorists.

• • •

In America, the Republican President Nixon was re-elected for a second term and the Watergate scandal broke.

• • •

Pakistan left the Commonwealth over Britain's decision to recognise the new state Bangladesh (formerly East Pakistan).

• • •

In Londonderry's Bogside district, 13 civilians were shot dead on 'Bloody Sunday'. In protest at the suspension of the Northern Irish Parliament and the imposition of direct rule from Westminster, the British Embassy in Dublin was burnt down.

• • •

In Britain, Ted Heath's Conservative government devalued the pound and introduced a freeze on wages and prices.

• • •

Refugees from Uganda, fleeing the regime of Idi Amin, began to arrive in Britain.

• • •

The American spacecraft Apollo 16 landed on the moon. A BEA Trident crashed at Heathrow airport, killing 117.

On May 28 the Duke of Windsor, who had reigned as King Edward VIII for 325 days in 1936 (the year of three Kings), died at his home in the Bois de Boulogne on the outskirts of Paris. The Duchess, for whom he had given up the throne, was with him. He was 77 and had been ill for some time. Ten days before his death the Queen and Prince Philip had visited him during a state visit to France, and when the Duchess came to Britain for the funeral service, she stayed at Buckingham Palace.

The service was held in St George's Chapel at Windsor. As the body rested in the chapel, thousands waited patiently to file past and pay their last respects, the queue winding its way around the castle walls. The Duchess of Windsor drove out from London the evening before the service to have her own time in the chapel. With her were the Prince of Wales and Earl Mountbatten of Burma. After the funeral she flew home to Paris.

In contrast to this sad and sombre occasion, with its unhappy memories, was the celebration of the Queen and Prince Philip's silver wedding. On November 20 huge crowds cheered the couple as they drove to Westminster Abbey for a service of Thanksgiving and then went on to Guildhall for a lunch given by the City of London. It was there the Queen delighted the guests with the self-mocking opening words of her speech: 'I think that everybody will concede that on this of

ABOVE *The Queen and Prince Philip with the Duchess of Windsor after the funeral service at St George's Chapel, Windsor, for her husband, the Duke of Windsor. He had abdicated in 1936 so that they could marry.*

all days I should begin my speech "My husband and I".'

The months before the anniversary had been particularly busy for the Queen with state visits: to France, Yugoslavia and Thailand, and tours of Singapore, Malaysia and islands in the Indian Ocean.

In the European context, the visit to France was both sensitive and significant, and the EEC was also much in mind when the Queen entertained Queen Juliana of the Netherlands, the Grand Duke of Luxembourg and the President of the German Federal Republic, all of whom paid state visits to Britain. At the banquet for the President she spoke strongly in favour of the Common Market, as she had done earlier in the year when in Paris. The bill clearing the way for Britain to enter the EEC in 1973 was approved in Parliament.

In August the Queen suffered a personal bereavement when Prince William of Gloucester, her cousin, was killed in a flying accident. Because of this the Queen cancelled a visit she was to have made to the Olympic Games in Munich, although Princess Anne was there to see Lt Mark Phillips help Britain's equestrian team win a gold medal in the Three Day Event. However, the Games were tragically overshadowed by the massacre of 11 Israeli athletes by Arab terrorists.

OPPOSITE *The Archbishop of Canterbury, Dr Michael Ramsey, pronounces the blessing at a service of Thanksgiving in Westminster Abbey to celebrate the silver wedding of the Queen and Prince Philip.*

1973

Tension between the West and the Soviet Union increased alarmingly when Egypt and Syria invaded Israel on the Day of Atonement.

•••

Britain, Denmark and the Republic of Ireland formally joined the EEC.

•••

The Vietnam peace agreement was signed in Paris.

•••

Greece proclaimed itself a republic; Archbishop Makarios was re-elected President of Cyprus; in the Philippines President Marcos extended his term in office 'indefinitely'.

•••

Juan Perón was again elected President of Argentina. The American Vice-President, Spiro Agnew, was forced to resign over the evasion of taxes. Chile's President Allende was murdered.

•••

As a result of OPEC quadrupling the price of oil, Britain experienced almost wartime restrictions. It also saw the introduction of VAT.

•••

In Britain, the Old Bailey and New Scotland Yard were among targets attacked by the IRA.

•••

The poet W.H. Auden, author J.R.R. Tolkien, and painter Pablo Picasso died.

•••

Commercial radio arrived in Britain.

PRINCESS ANNE MARRIES

A year that was to end with Britain experiencing the sort of restrictions normally associated only with wartime began on an optimistic high – at least for pro-Europeans. Britain, together with Denmark and the Republic of Ireland, joined the Common Market, and to mark the occasion the Queen and Prince Philip attended Fanfare for Europe, a gala performance at the Royal Opera House, Covent Garden.

Later in the year, on November 14, many millions of viewers took time off to watch the wedding of Princess Anne and Captain Mark Phillips in Westminster Abbey. Their engagement had finally been announced in May, after much press speculation and an ill-advised denial by the then Press Secretary at Buckingham Palace. Lt Phillips, as he was at the time, was a commoner, a serving soldier and an Olympic three-day eventer. Apart from the Queen herself, no member of the royal family marrying since the war had married royalty and most people in Britain seemed to approve. It was a double celebration for the Archbishop of Canterbury, who conducted the marriage, and for Prince Charles – it was also their birthday.

OPPOSITE *Princess
Anne and Captain
Mark Phillips, with
their families, in the
Throne Room at
Buckingham Palace
after their marriage in
Westminster Abbey.*

ABOVE *A romantic
picture in an historic
setting. The newly wed
Princess Anne and
Mark Phillips pose in
the Long Gallery at
Windsor Castle.*

There was much royal activity during the year. The Queen and Prince Philip went twice to Canada, the second time for the Commonwealth Heads of Government conference in Ottawa – the first such meeting that the Queen had attended outside London.

The royal couple also went to Australia where the Queen opened the spectacular Sydney Opera House. It was a short visit undertaken specifically for that purpose, and the idea of the Queen 'popping over' went down well down under. The Presidents of Mexico and Zaire paid state visits; the President of Mexico stayed with the Queen at Windsor Castle.

The royal visits to Canada helped to clarify to Canadians the Queen's role in the government of their country. Canada was one of the former British possessions which, on attaining independence, had chosen to remain a constitutional monarchy with the Queen as head of state. South of the Canadian border the Watergate hearings in Washington were being shown live and prime-time to the world, and many Canadians were reassured that their own system had many advantages. Talk of abolishing the monarchy in Canada was heard much less than had been the case during earlier visits by the Queen. The French-Canadian Prime Minister Pierre Trudeau invariably spoke warmly of *'la Reine du Canada'*.

A lack of humanity and compassion can be very destructive – how easily this causes divisions within nations and between nations. We should remember instead how much we have in common and resolve to give expression to the best of our human qualities, not only at Christmas, but right through the year.

Extract from The Queen's Christmas Message

LEFT *The Queen, Baroness Spencer-Churchill and Mr Winston Churchill MP at the unveiling, by the Baroness, of the bronze statue of Sir Winston Churchill in Parliament Square, London. It is the work of Ivor Robert-Jones.*

KIDNAP ATTEMPT ON PRINCESS ANNE

KEY EVENTS

Valéry Giscard d'Estaing was elected President of France.

• • •

Greece voted to abolish the monarchy.

• • •

A cyclone devastated the Australian city of Darwin.

• • •

An IRA campaign to bomb mainland Britain resulted in two bomb explosions in London and others at public houses in Guildford, Woolwich and Birmingham. A bomb in Oxford Street was timed to hit Christmas shoppers. Altogether some 30 people were killed, and many others injured.

• • •

In Northern Ireland, the power-sharing executive that had replaced direct rule from Westminster was brought down by the extreme Unionists.

• • •

In Britain, 28 people were killed and many others injured when an explosion destroyed a chemical plant at Flixborough in Lincolnshire.

The year 1974 was to demonstrate once again the sheer staying power of the Queen and the stability a constitutional monarchy provides. At the beginning of the year Richard Nixon was President of the United States, Georges Pompidou was President of France, Juan Perón was President of Argentina, Willy Brandt was Chancellor of the German Federal Republic, Golda Meir was Prime Minister of Israel, Haile Selassie was Emperor of Ethiopia and Edward Heath was Prime Minister of Britain. By the year's end not one was still in power. Disgrace, death, revolution and the democratic process had taken their toll.

RIGHT *Princess Anne grew up sharing her father's love of sailing and was for many years a regular visitor to the regatta at Cowes, on the Isle of Wight.*

ABOVE *The Queen*
waits to present
medals during the
Commonwealth Games
held at Christchurch,
New Zealand.

ABOVE *The royal car in the Mall soon after the failed attempt by Ian Ball to kidnap Princess Anne. His car is in front.*

In the United States President Richard Nixon, faced with impeachment for 'high crimes and misdemeanours', chose to resign. He was succeeded by Gerald Ford, who had been appointed Vice-President when Spiro Agnew had resigned after admitting tax evasion offences. In turn Ford appointed Nelson Rockefeller to be his Vice-President.

At home a general election was held on February 28. The Queen was in Australia at the time, but flew home immediately when she learned that no party had an overall majority. After a weekend spent trying, unsuccessfully, to persuade the Liberals to join the Conservatives in a coalition, Edward Heath resigned and the Queen sent for Harold Wilson. Labour was back in power. A second general election in October gave Labour a clear lead over the Conservatives and an overall majority of three.

After the February election and while the new government was sorting out the industrial crisis (a national miners' strike; a three-day working week; power cuts) the Queen left London to resume her interrupted tour, arriving in Bali on time for a state visit to Indonesia. The royal party was staying in Jakarta, in Java, when the Queen was woken one night to be told of a terrifying attempt to kidnap Princess Anne as she and her husband were driving along the Mall towards Buckingham Palace.

Thanks to the coolness of Princess Anne and her husband, and to the bravery of members of the police and passers-by, the attempt to kidnap the Princess was frustrated, but not before shots had been fired. The would-be kidnapper,

26-year-old Ian Ball (who was later committed to a psychiatric hospital for an indefinite period), had driven a car across the front of the royal limousine, forcing it to stop, and had tried to haul the Princess into his vehicle. His plan was to demand a £3,000,000 ransom. The Princess's police officer, Inspector Jim Beaton, her driver, and Mr McConnell, a passing journalist who went to help, were all injured. So too was PC Edmonds when he arrived at the scene. The Princess herself was shaken but unharmed and was able to reassure her parents there was no need for them to return home. The Princess, Mark Phillips and Inspector Beaton were all later honoured for their coolness and bravery, and the Inspector received the George Cross.

Earlier in the year Prince Philip had opened, in January, the Commonwealth Games in Christchurch, New Zealand, where he was later joined by the Queen, Princess Anne and Mark Phillips for the closing stages.

That same month Princess Margaret paid the first visit to Cyprus by a member of the royal family and Earl Mountbatten of Burma broke the ice for the royals when he spent a week in Communist China. Princess Margaret's host, President Makarios, was later ousted in a military coup. He had long been a thorn in the side of British governments.

For the entire royal family there was great sadness when the Queen's uncle, the Duke of Gloucester, died at the age of 74. He was survived by his younger son, Prince Richard, who inherited the title, and by his wife, who took the title of Princess Alice, Duchess of Gloucester.

Among the Queen's visitors were the Queen of Denmark and, for lunch just before Christmas, the Prime Minister of Australia, Gough Whitlam, and Mrs Whitlam. Christmas itself was as usual spent at Windsor, but Sandringham House had the builders in, so for the New Year the Queen and Prince Philip stayed at Wood Farm, a six-bedroom farmhouse on the Sandringham estate.

BELOW *The Duke of Gloucester, the Queen's last surviving uncle, died on October 6. He was seventy-four and had been ill for six years.*

Goodwill is better than resentment, tolerance is better than revenge, compassion is better than anger, above all a lively concern for the interests of others as well as our own. In times of doubt and anxiety the attitudes people show in their daily lives, in their homes, and in their work, are of supreme importance.

Extract from The Queen's Christmas Message

1975

Spain restored the monarchy two days after the death of the Fascist dictator General Franco.

• • •

In Britain, the Conservative party elected Mrs Margaret Thatcher to be its first woman leader. The Sex Discrimination and Equal Pay Acts came into force.

• • •

In the House of Commons a free vote on capital punishment resulted in a majority of 129 against its reintroduction.

• • •

Terrorism continued in Northern Ireland. The number of violent deaths since 1969 rose to 1,300. Well over 12,000 had been injured, many severely. On the mainland bomb attacks continued against both people and property.

• • •

A referendum on whether Britain should stay in the EEC resulted in 17,378,581 voters saying 'Yes' and 8,470,073 saying 'No'.

• • •

Dutch elm disease ravaged the English countryside.

• • •

King Faisal of Saudi Arabia was assassinated.

OPPOSITE *'When in Rome . . .' or, in this case, Japan. The Queen is shoeless as she prepares to enter a temple in Kyoto during her state visit in May.*

A WOMAN'S WORLD

*P*arliament approved a further rise in the Civil List. Responding to the inflation rate, the annual allowance to the Queen as head of state and to other members of the royal family was raised from £980 to £1.4 million. The Queen herself agreed to add a further £150,000 from her own sources.

The day that Parliament approved the increases was the day that Mrs Margaret Thatcher made her first appearance in the House of Commons as leader of the Opposition. On this occasion she and the Prime Minister, Harold Wilson, were in complete agreement concerning the value of the monarchy in general and of the Queen in particular.

There was a constitutional crisis in Australia when, in an unprecedented move, the Queen's representative, Governor-General Sir John Kerr, sacked the Prime Minister, Gough Whitlam, who had failed to get the approval of Parliament for government expenditure. Although the Queen was not involved in the decision – she was informed only after the event – the Governor-General's action did call into question the role of the monarchy in Australia.

In a busy year of travel, the Queen and Prince Philip were twice in the Caribbean – visiting Bermuda, the Bahamas and Barbados in February, and Jamaica in April, where the Queen attended the meeting of Commonwealth Heads of Government. The royal couple also went to Mexico and Hong Kong, made a private visit to Honolulu and, for the first time, a state visit to Japan. It was 30 years since the end of the Second World War. The royal couple drew large crowds but there was little cheering or clapping; most spectators were too busy with their cameras!

In February the Prince of Wales, with his cousin the Duke of Gloucester and Earl Mountbatten, visited New Delhi and Kathmandu, where the Prince represented the Queen at the coronation of King Birendra of Nepal (who had succeeded his father in 1972). Mountbatten, the last Viceroy of India, particularly enjoyed showing the two young men 'his' part of the world.

The Prince went to Canada in April; at the same time Princess Anne and her husband were in Australia. With air travel now so much quicker, there were no longer the gaps between royal visits to Australia that had marked the earlier years of the reign. Canada was also being visited regularly, as the different Provinces celebrated their centennials.

The Queen received visits from the King of Spain and President Julius Nyerere of Tanzania. Other engagements for the Queen included a visit to Greenwich to mark the centenary of the Royal Observatory, and opening the new Covent Garden market in south London. Significantly for the economy of the country, the Queen also inaugurated the flow of British North Sea oil at Dyce, near Aberdeen.

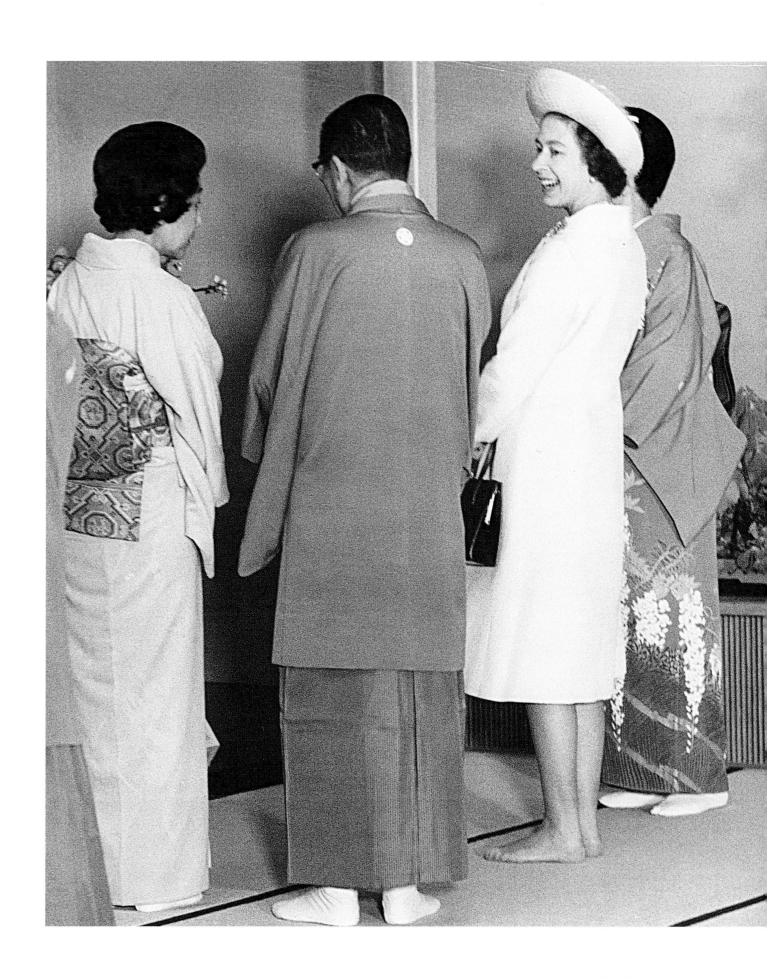

BELOW *An unexpected
customer stops at a
vegetable stall during
the royal tour of Hong
Kong. The Queen and
Prince Philip spent
three days in the colony,
en route for Japan.*

*It does matter [therefore] what each individual
does each day. Kindness, sympathy, resolution and
courteous behaviour are infectious. Acts of courage
and self-sacrifice, like those of the people who
refuse to be terrorized by kidnappers or hijackers,
or those who defuse bombs, are an inspiration
to others.*

Extract from The Queen's Christmas Message

1976

CELEBRATIONS IN THE UNITED STATES

KEY EVENTS

Americans celebrated 200 years of independence and elected a former peanut farmer from Georgia, Jimmy Carter, president.

•••

In South Africa, anti-apartheid riots in Soweto led to bloodshed.

•••

Britain and Iceland brought the 'cod war' to an end.

•••

Concorde began commercial transatlantic flights and the United States' space shuttle made its first test flight.

•••

In Britain, this was the year of the long, hot summer and of the great drought.

•••

Chairman Mao, the leader of Communist China, and his second-in-command, Chou En-Lai, died. The British wartime hero Field Marshal Viscount Montgomery of Alamein died, as did the crime writer Agatha Christie, and painter L.S. Lowry.

'Come home, all is forgiven', was the slogan used by British Airways (in the ample shape of Robert Morley) to entice Americans to Britain during the year of the United States' bicentennial celebrations. It caught the mood as the United States, with Gerald Ford in the White House, celebrated with a very good party indeed.

It was appropriate that the Queen should visit Britain's former colonies on this occasion, but not on Independence Day itself. July 4 was a day for Americans with, in New York, open-air concerts in Central Park, tall ships off the Battery, and thousands of fireworks.

President and Mrs Ford proved generous hosts when the Queen and Prince Philip did arrive to spend several days in the east coast cities of Philadelphia, Boston and New York, and, of course, Washington DC. The welcome they received was warm and good-natured, even in Boston, where the Irish seemed as pleased to see the royal couple as anyone else.

Immediately before their visit to the United States the Queen and Prince Philip had been in Canada where they and their two younger sons attended the

RIGHT The Chief of the Union of New Brunswick Indians petitions the Queen during her visit to Canada's Maritime Provinces. The complaint was that a royal proclamation of 1763, granting various rights to the tribe, had not been honoured.

OPPOSITE *To mark his resignation as Prime Minister, Harold Wilson invited the Queen to a farewell dinner. Here she is welcomed at Number 10.*

LEFT *The Queen dances with her host, President Ford, at the state banquet held in the White House during the Bi-centennial State Visit.*

BELOW *Not what it seems. The Queen is **not** leaving one of her prisons on day release, but visiting a somewhat unlikely stand at Badminton Horse Trials.*

Montreal Olympic Games. Princess Anne was a member of the British equestrian team and was competing in the Three Day Event. However, she failed to win a medal in spite of the support of Captain Mark Phillips and her family. Prince Andrew and Prince Edward enjoyed the Olympic experience, particularly when the Scot, David Wilkie, won a gold for Britain in the Olympic pool.

The royal party also visited Nova Scotia and New Brunswick on Canada's eastern seaboard.

Two other significant events took place this year. In March Princess Margaret and Lord Snowdon announced that their marriage was over and that they were to separate. The same week the Prime Minister, Harold Wilson, in good health and seemingly still enjoying life in Number 10, formally tendered his resignation to the Queen. He had in fact told her of his intention some months earlier but to the public the news came as a complete surprise.

The Labour party had immediately to elect a new leader. James Callaghan was unlike his predecessor in many ways but shared Harold Wilson's support of the monarchy. As a former Chancellor of the Exchequer, Home Secretary and Foreign Secretary, Jim Callaghan was already well known to the Queen.

The Queen and Prince Philip also went to Finland in May and to Luxembourg in November. President Geisel of Brazil came to Britain and so too did the new French President, Valéry Giscard d'Estaing. This was the first time the two heads of state had met since the President had taken office and in the European context it was crucially important to keep the old entente as cordiale as possible. The Queen played a significant role in this.

At the end of the year Prince Charles left full-time naval service in order to undertake more royal duties.

A Splendid Silver Jubilee

KEY EVENTS

Leonid Brezhnev became President of the USSR.

• • •

Spain held its first democratic elections for 41 years.

• • •

Menachem Begin became Prime Minister of Israel. Peace talks began between Israel and Egypt.

• • •

In India, Mrs Indira Gandhi was defeated in the general election, and was later arrested on corruption charges.

• • •

In Pakistan, Zulfikar Bhutto's People's party won the general election but four months later he was arrested in a military takeover.

• • •

The number of unemployed in Britain reached a million.

• • •

The Muslim mosque in London's Regents Park was officially opened.

• • •

Lord Avon, the former Prime Minister Sir Anthony Eden, died. Elvis Presley, Groucho Marx, Maria Callas, Sir Charles Chaplin and Bing Crosby also died.

*his was the Queen's year. For months, almost overwhelmed at times, she smiled her way around the world.

The statistics are daunting: 56,000 miles around the South Pacific, New Zealand, Australia, Canada and the Caribbean; 36 counties visited in Great Britain and Northern Ireland; cards, messages, gifts by the tens of thousands. She and Prince Philip travelled by plane (Concorde on the last leg from Barbados to London), by royal train, in the royal yacht, by car and on foot through the crowds to meet her people. It was hugely appreciated and had the effect of unifying the country and the Commonwealth once again.

Cold figures alone, though, tell nothing of the real story. It was not just a time for formal state occasions; the Queen's Silver Jubilee was celebrated by millions, throughout the United Kingdom and the Commonwealth, who wanted to show their affection for the Queen – huge crowds (of people of all ages) who turned out to express feelings that went far beyond respect and admiration. We love you, Liz! banners might not be to everyone's taste but that is exactly the sentiment so many were expressing.

'Liz' was overwhelmed. 'I had no idea,' was one reaction, echoing the genuinely modest surprise of her grandfather, George V, at the time of his Silver Jubilee.

During the planning stage for these extraordinary months some had been

RIGHT *Jubilee Year encapsulated: flags, flowers, children and smiles all the way, throughout the United Kingdom.*

ABOVE *A salute from Concorde as the Queen and Prince Philip, on* HMS Britannia, *approach Barbados on the last leg of the Silver Jubilee tour. They returned to London on the aircraft.*

unsure of the response in the United Kingdom and the Commonwealth to such celebrations and their cost. Typically, the Queen herself was cautious, wishing to avoid extravagance – a view that was shared by Prime Minister Jim Callaghan and Home Secretary Roy Jenkins. However, advisors who were more in touch got it right, judging that the country and the Commonwealth would wish to show their gratitude to the Queen for 25 years of service, and were definitely ready for a darn good party. And that is exactly what they had, in thousands of villages, streets and avenues across the world.

There were national celebrations, too, not least on Jubilee Day itself. In London, there was the procession to St Paul's Cathedral before the service of Thanksgiving; the walk to the Guildhall; the appearances on the Palace balcony to crowds massed far down the Mall; bonfires, fireworks, and a pageant on the Thames.

Meanwhile, the leaders of the western world (including the new American President, Jimmy Carter) and of the Commonwealth were in town for summit meetings and conferences. And when she replied to a loyal address from both Houses of Parliament in Westminster Hall, the Queen clearly had the possibility of devolution in mind when she said she could not help but recall that she had been crowned Queen of the United Kingdom.

BELOW *A first-ever flight in a helicopter took the Queen on her first visit to Northern Ireland for eleven years.*

Nowhere is reconciliation more desperately needed than in Northern Ireland. That is why I was particularly pleased to go there. No-one dared to promise an early end to the troubles but there is no doubt that people of goodwill in Northern Ireland were greatly heartened by the chance they had to share the celebrations with the rest of the nation and the Commonwealth.

Extract from The Queen's Christmas Message

LEFT *The christening of Peter Phillips, son of Princess Anne and Captain Phillips, and the Queen's first grandchild.*

As the Queen toured the Commonwealth countries the reception was the same. Whether against the background of the great opera house and bridge in Sydney, Australia, or in the bustling square in the centre of Bridgetown, Barbados, the crowds were there. And it was so personal. Many of those with republican views had no problem at all in thanking the Queen for the years of service. In her own speeches the Queen constantly expressed her gratitude for the support she had received over the 25 years of her reign.

At home the Queen opened the new underground line to Heathrow airport, watched Virginia Wade win the Ladies Singles' title at Wimbledon, and enjoyed with Prince Philip the delight of becoming grandparents. Peter Mark Andrew Phillips was born to Princess Anne and Captain Mark Phillips on November 15. He was to prove a great joy to his grandparents, as were the other grandchildren in due course.

In October, as planned, the Queen's Private Secretary, Sir Martin Charteris, retired after what the Queen described as a 'lifetime' of service to her. He had been in Kenya with her when she became Queen, and had been, as he himself would say, 'in love in the most proper sense' with her since well before that. He was a remarkable man, witty and wise, who served the Queen wonderfully well. He was succeeded by Philip Moore, a man with a very different style but equally effective.

During the Jubilee Year the Prince of Wales was in charge of the Queen's Jubilee Appeal which eventually raised £16 million, the money going to 'help young people help others'.

PRINCE CHARLES AT THIRTY

KEY EVENTS

In Rhodesia a timetable was at last agreed for independence under black majority rule.

•••

Russia and Afghanistan signed a friendship treaty. China and the United States resumed diplomatic relations.

•••

In Britain, the proceedings of the House of Commons were broadcast for the first time on radio.

•••

A strike over the use of new technology brought publication of The Times to a halt.

•••

The world's first 'test-tube baby', Louise Brown, was born in Manchester.

•••

Pope Paul VI died of a heart attack. After only 33 days his successor, John Paul I, also died. The third Pope of the year, the first Pole ever to hold the office, took the name John Paul II. The Archbishop of Canterbury attended the investiture – the first such move since the break with the Roman Catholic Church in the 16th century.

*S*ilver Jubilee Year was inevitably a hard act to follow but in its own way 1978 was busy enough. The Queen and Prince Philip entertained at Buckingham Palace both President Eanes of Portugal and, with less pleasure, President Ceaucescu of Romania whose despotic style of government were already recognised, but whose semi-independence from the Soviet bloc was felt to be worth supporting. The Queen was particularly irritated during his stay by his insistence on retreating to the Palace gardens to talk to his staff because he feared his rooms were bugged.

In May the Queen and Prince Philip paid a successful and well-received state visit to West Germany and in the summer, joined by Prince Andrew and Prince Edward, were in Canada to attend the Commonwealth Games. Their visit took in other parts of Alberta where the warmth of their welcome was clearly demonstrated.

The Prince of Wales celebrated his 30th birthday in November with a Palace party but without committing himself to any of the young ladies regularly put forward by Fleet Street as 'the next Queen'. Two weddings did take place, however. Princess Margaret and Lord Snowdon divorced by common consent in May after two years' separation, and Lord Snowdon married Miss Lucy Lindsay-Hogg. The Queen did not attend the ceremony. Nor did she attend the wedding in Vienna of her cousin, Prince Michael of Kent, and Baroness Marie-Christine von Reibnitz. The bride was Roman Catholic, and in spite of the couple indicating that any children would be brought up in the Church of England, Prince Michael had to renounce his place in the line of succession.

RIGHT *Earning their parachute wings in harness. The Prince of Wales and Prince Andrew underwent a two-week training course at RAF Brize Norton in April.*

As for Prince Charles, a varied programme during the year included representing the Queen at the funerals of President Kenyatta of Kenya and of Sir Robert Menzies, the former Prime Minister of Australia. He also opened the new Gatwick airport buildings and attended a Salvation Army congress at Wembley Stadium.

He and Prince Andrew, who was on his Easter holiday from Gordonstoun, took a parachute course and gained their 'wings'. 1978 was the 60th anniversary of the formation of the RAF and the Queen and Prince Philip attended a special service in Westminster Abbey to mark the occasion.

BELOW *The Queen rides in a state carriage with President Ceaucescu when the Romanian dictator paid a state visit in June.*

IRA MURDER EARL MOUNTBATTEN

Rhodesia voted for black majority rule and for a change of name to Zimbabwe; and the former Prime Minister of Pakistan, Zulfikar Bhutto, was hanged. The Shah of Iran was forced into permanent exile and Ayatollah Khomeini assumed the leadership.

•••

There were signs of hope in the Middle East, where Israel and Egypt signed a peace treaty. In Uganda, President Idi Amin was finally removed from power.

•••

In Britain, the year began with industrial strife, and in March Prime Minister James Callaghan advised the Queen to dissolve Parliament. In the general election the Tories were voted back into power and Mrs Thatcher moved into 10 Downing Street.

•••

The Times newspaper eventually reappeared after industrial action lasting nearly a year.

•••

Gracie Fields and the veteran American film star John Wayne died.

On May 3 the Conservatives won a majority over Labour in the general election. On May 4 the Queen appointed the United Kingdom's first woman Prime Minister, Margaret Thatcher. It was, in its way, momentous but for many people, the Queen included, industrial disputes, politics and the passions they aroused were all put into perspective by two acts of IRA terrorism.

Just before the election got under way the Conservative spokesman on Northern Ireland, Airey Neave, was murdered when a bomb placed in his car exploded as he was driving away from the underground car park of the House of Commons.

On August Bank Holiday tragedy struck again, this time directly involving the Queen and her family. Lord Mountbatten of Burma (Uncle Dickie to the royal family); one of his grandsons, Nicholas Knatchbull; the Dowager Lady Brabourne, mother-in-law of his daughter, Patricia; and a young Irish crewman were all killed when a bomb planted on their boat and detonated by IRA terrorists on shore

RIGHT *The Queen and Prince Philip lead the mourners at the funeral service of Earl Mountbatten of Burma in Westminster Abbey.*

ABOVE *Soon after becoming Prime Minister, Margaret Thatcher attended the Commonwealth Conference in Lusaka where the Queen hosted a dinner for the heads of government.*

exploded as they were leaving for a fishing trip from Mullaghmore, County Sligo in the Irish Republic. Several others in the party were badly injured. The Queen made no public statement but her grief was apparent to all at the Earl's funeral in Westminster Abbey. He was a cousin of her grandfather, George V, uncle of Prince Philip, and an especially close friend and confidante to Prince Charles.

That same Bank Holiday 18 British soldiers on duty on the border at Warrenpoint, County Down in Northern Ireland were killed when an IRA landmine exploded. Many were members of the Parachute Regiment whose Colonel-in-Chief is the Prince of Wales. Already devastated by the death of Earl Mountbatten, the Prince had to face the shock of this second appalling atrocity. It was a terrible day.

Courageously, a Mountbatten family wedding nevertheless went ahead in October when the late Earl's grandson, Lord Romsey, married Penelope Eastwood. The groom's parents had been on board the boat at Mullaghmore and were still in wheelchairs as a result of their injuries. The Queen and many other members of the royal family were at the wedding, adding support to a family event overshadowed by tragedy.

LEFT *The smile, the bouquet – such a picture could have been taken in so many different places. On this occasion the Queen was arriving in Zambia.*

For the Queen there was another, less harrowing but nevertheless difficult situation to deal with when her former art expert, Sir Anthony Blunt, was named as the fourth man in the Burgess-Maclean-Philby spy scandal. Blunt had admitted his spying activities to British security in 1964 but had worked for the Queen for a number of years after that. Now he was deprived of his knighthood.

The Queen and Prince Philip made a state visit to Denmark in May, where Queen Margrethe and Prince Henrik were the hosts. This was followed by over two weeks in Africa in July, when the royal couple spent time in Tanzania, Malawi, Botswana and Zambia, strengthening links between the United Kingdom and the Commonwealth. The Commonwealth Heads of Government conference in Lusaka, which followed, was the first Mrs Thatcher had attended; she did not always seem to share the Queen's enthusiasm for the institution.

It is an unhappy coincidence that political and economic forces have made this an exceptionally difficult and tragic year for many families and children in several parts of the world – but particularly in South-East Asia. The situation has created a desperately serious challenge and I am glad to know that so many people of the Commonwealth have responded with wonderful generosity and kindness.

Extract from The Queen's Christmas Message

1980

KEY EVENTS

In two Commonwealth countries two former prime ministers returned to power: Pierre Trudeau in Canada and Mrs Indira Gandhi in India.

• • •

Princess Beatrix was installed as Queen of the Netherlands after her mother, Queen Juliana, abdicated on her 71st birthday.

• • •

Robert Mugabe was elected Prime Minister of Zimbabwe after defeating both Joshua Nkomo and the former white leader of the former Rhodesia, Ian Smith.

• • •

Polish ship workers in the solidarity movement led by Lech Walensa won the right to form trade unions.

• • •

A disaster in the North Sea led to 123 deaths when a mobile oil rig capsized and sank.

• • •

In London, the SAS successfully stormed the Iranian embassy to free hostages held by Iranian terrorists demanding the release of political prisoners at home.

• • •

Yugoslavia's President Tito died, and the former Beatle John Lennon was shot dead outside his home in New York. Sir Cecil Beaton, Graham Sutherland, Alfred Hitchcock, Peter Sellers, Sir Billy Butlin and the British Fascist leader Sir Oswald Mosley also died.

LADY DIANA SPENCER ENTERS THE SCENE

*O*n August 4 some two million people turned out to form what was described as 'a human corridor of affection' as Queen Elizabeth, the Queen Mother was driven in the 1902 state landau to St Paul's Cathedral for a service of Thanksgiving on her 80th birthday.

The Queen Mother, a great-grandmother since the birth of Peter Phillips, had long since established herself as part of the nation's 'family' – an 'honorary grandmother' to millions.

The Queen and the others in the royal family were delighted to step back from the limelight on this special day. Princes Charles, the first grandchild and always very close to the Queen Mother who had looked after him so often as a small child when his parents were abroad, was her proud escort for the anniversary. The Queen Mother herself, alert and as involved as ever, clearly loved every moment of her day.

The Prince, too, had his own special day, as an author, with the publication of his book *The Old Man of Lochnagar*. The fantasy, set in the beautiful highlands and lakes around Balmoral Castle, had originally been thought up to entertain the Prince's young brothers. It was illustrated by Sir Hugh Casson and has since been translated into more than a dozen different languages.

Nothing, it seemed, could take speculation about Prince Charles' future wife off the front pages of the newspapers, but the field was rapidly narrowing down to just one young woman. Lady Diana Spencer's name was common currency, her picture published at every possible opportunity, and her life already being lived in the proverbial goldfish bowl. Although nothing was official, royal 'experts' in the

OPPOSITE *Some months before her engagement, Lady Diana Spencer (right) and Camilla Parker Bowles were at Ludlow Racecourse to watch Prince Charles compete in an Amateurs Handicap Race.*

ABOVE *It clearly was a very happy birthday indeed; August 4 and the Queen Mother is a mere 80 years old!*

We face grave problems in the life of our country, but our predecessors, and many alive today, have faced far greater difficulties, both in peace and war, and have overcome them by courage and calm determination. They never lost hope and they never lacked confidence in themselves or in their children.

Extract from The Queen's Christmas Message

media were of one mind as to who might become the next Queen.

The Queen's two younger sons were busy with their own lives. Prince Andrew was in the Royal Navy on a short service commission as a Seaman Officer specialising as a helicopter pilot. He passed out from the Britannia Royal Naval College at Dartmouth in April, following in the footsteps of his brother, father and grandfather. In November he was posted to the Royal Naval air station at Culdrose.

Prince Edward celebrated his 16th birthday in March. He was in his third year at Gordonstoun where, among other activities, he was a member of the school's ATC. He took gliding lessons and, having earned his gliding wings, began powered aeroplane lessons at RAF Lossiemouth in October. He took part in several sports and was also doing well academically.

Illustrating a different approach to maintaining a constitutional monarchy, Queen Juliana of the Netherlands announced that she would be abdicating in favour of her daughter Beatrix. Her own mother, Queen Wilhelmina, had also passed on the baton while she was still alive.

The Union flag came down in Africa for the last time when the former colony of Rhodesia emerged as the Republic of Zimbabwe under the leadership of President Mugabe.

BELOW *The Queen in Marrakech with her host King Hassan during her state visit to Morocco.*

1981

'THE STUFF OF WHICH FAIRY TALES ARE MADE'

KEY EVENTS

Ronald Reagan was sworn in as President of the United States in January. Ten weeks later he was shot and wounded as he was leaving a Washington hotel.
Pope John Paul II was shot and wounded in his 'Popemobile' in Rome.

•••

President Anwar Sadat of Egypt was assassinated while taking the salute at a military parade in Cairo.

•••

François Mitterand was elected President of France, and Dr Garrett Fitzgerald took office as Prime Minister in the Irish Republic.

•••

In Britain, Michael Foot became the leader of a divided Labour party: four former members of Labour administrations (the 'Gang of Four') had launched the Social Democratic party (SDP).

•••

Racial violence broke out in some inner-city districts, notably Toxteth in Liverpool and Brixton in south London.

•••

Peter Sutcliffe, the 'Yorkshire Ripper', pleaded guilty to killing 13 women during a four-year period.

RIGHT *The Queen's formal approval was needed for Prince Charles and Lady Diana Spencer to marry. It was given happily.*

$\mathcal{O}$n Wednesday July 29 the entire world, it seemed, took part in a wedding. Hundreds of millions of people around the world shared in the happiness of the couple and their families as Lady Diana Spencer and HRH The Prince of Wales married in St Paul's Cathedral.

A beautiful young aristocrat, Lady Diana Spencer had captivated the world's media and through it the world's readers and viewers. At just 20 she was already well on the way to being the most photographed woman in the world. The Prince, at 32, had lost his status as the most eligible bachelor in the world but in exchange had, as one paper put it, 'the wife to dream of'.

He had proposed to Diana early in February and the official announcement of the engagement had been issued on February 24 when the happy couple faced the press in the garden of Buckingham Palace. Asked by the Press Association's court correspondent whether they were in love, Diana instantly replied, 'Of course!' Prince Charles added the curious caveat, 'Whatever "in love" means.'

For the next five months wedding talk dominated the tabloid headlines and

LEFT *A memorable moment on a memorable day – the balcony kiss.*

ABOVE *The newly married Prince and Princess of Wales leave St Paul's Cathedral to be greeted again by tens of thousands of well-wishers.*

there were times when the pressure seemed too much for Lady Diana to cope with. Cope she did, just, but on the day itself all worries and anxieties were set aside as she drove from the Queen Mother's home, Clarence House, to St Paul's Cathedral, wearing a dress with an immensely long train. Her father, Earl Spencer, escorted her with great dignity despite the effects of an earlier stroke. Lady Diana's mother and stepmother were both in the congregation, and Prince Charles had his two brothers as his 'supporters'.

When the couple emerged at the head of the Cathedral steps it was as the Prince and Princess of Wales, their marriage having been described by the Archbishop of Canterbury in his sermon as 'the stuff of which fairy tales are made'.

The procession along the long route from St Paul's to Buckingham Palace took them past more than half a million well wishers, with the crowds pouring along the Mall to mass outside the palace railings. The balcony appearances, and 'the kiss', perfectly rounded off the celebrations. The couple began their honeymoon at the Mountbattens' home, Broadlands in Hampshire, before cruising in the royal yacht *Britannia* in the Mediterranean.

Just over a month earlier the Queen had an unnerving experience during the annual Trooping the Colour parade to mark her official birthday. As she was riding Burmese along the Mall on her way to Horseguards Parade six shots were fired from among the watching crowd. Fortunately they were blanks but it was a horrifying moment. As police ran forward and her escort closed around her, the Queen calmed Burmese and rode on, apparently unshaken. An unemployed young man, Marcus Sargeant, was detained, charged and imprisoned.

BELOW *Startled, as well she might have been, the Queen keeps her horse, Burmese, under control after blank shots were fired in the Mall during the Trooping the Colour parade.*

On May 15 Princess Anne gave birth to a daughter, Zara.

In addition to the members of other royal families and other heads of state who had been invited to the wedding of the Prince and Princess of Wales, there were two state visits during the year as well: the President of Nigeria came in March and King Khalid of Saudi Arabia in June. The Queen and Prince Philip visited Norway in May, then parts of Australia and New Zealand before going to Sri Lanka in October. The Australian 'leg' also took in the Commonwealth Heads of Government meeting in Melbourne.

WAR IN THE SOUTH ATLANTIC

$\mathcal{B}$etween April and June the United Kingdom found itself once more at war, this time with Argentina. Initially, the Argentine invasion of the British-owned Falkland Islands in the South Atlantic was seen as something of a national humiliation, and the Foreign Secretary, Lord Carrington, resigned for having misread the warning signs. The Falklands had been a Crown colony since 1832, and Argentina's justification for the invasion was to reclaim the Malvinas (as they were known in Spanish) for the Argentines. When large numbers of Argentine troops landed on the islands on April 2 the British Governor, Rex Hunt, ordered the small contingent of Royal Marines at Port Stanley to surrender.

Britain declared war, and in the ensuing weeks the Government assembled a large task force (navy, army and air), moved it 8,000 miles south and went into action. Argentine bases were only 400 miles away. By the time the Argentines surrendered in Port Stanley on June 14 the death toll for the whole campaign was given as 255 Britons and 652 Argentines. Many more on both sides were seriously wounded.

The Falklands war concerned the Queen greatly, both for the safety of the servicemen and women of her fighting forces and for the anxiety of the families at home. This time, however, she and Prince Philip were also personally involved. Prince Andrew, a naval helicopter pilot serving on HMS *Invincible*, was in direct action and his life, too, was at risk.

The support of the United States' Government in applying sanctions against Argentina undoubtedly helped the war effort, and President and Mrs Reagan were

ABOVE *Prince Andrew, back from active service in the Falklands, with his parents and sister on his ship, HMS* Invincible.

OPPOSITE *An early morning ride at Windsor for the Queen and her guest, President Reagan.*

guests of the Queen at Windsor Castle while the fighting was still going on. The visit had been planned before the invasion, but the timing was appropriate.

The Queen was to experience yet another personal shock when she was awoken in her bedroom in Buckingham Palace on the morning of July 9. Sitting on her bed, having broken into the Palace, wandered around, helped himself to some wine and entered the bedroom, was a total stranger: Michael Fagan. He talked for some minutes and asked for a cigarette before the Queen was able to summon help. Not surprisingly, there was a major reassessment of security at the Palace, while Fagan was charged, not with lese-majesty, but with theft of wine while trespassing.

The breach of security, a serious one in any circumstances, was taken additionally seriously in view of the Provisional IRA activity in mainland Britain. The acts of terrorism in Ulster continued remorselessly while their campaign moved into central London again, with two attacks in royal parks on July 20. In Hyde Park a car bomb exploded as a detachment of the Queen's Household Cavalry, the Royals and Blues, rode along the South Carriage Road. Two guardsmen were killed and six bystanders were injured. Seven of the horses also died. Less than three hours later a bomb placed under a bandstand in Regents Park went off, killing 6 army bandsmen and injuring 24 more, all members of the Royal Green Jackets. As with all such outrages, the Queen was deeply distressed. The messages of condolence that she sent might have appeared somewhat formal but they came from the heart.

The day after these attacks, on July 21, the Queen and Prince Philip became grandparents again, when the Princess of Wales gave birth to Prince William in St Mary's Hospital, Paddington. The baby became second in the line of succession after his father.

In April the Queen and Prince Philip had visited Canada for a Repatriation Ceremony in Ottawa, when the Queen transferred sovereignty of the 1867 Canadian Constitution from Britain to Canada. It was a formality but an important one for Canadians. The royal couple also went to Australia in October for the Commonwealth Games in Brisbane, and then on to Papua New Guinea and other islands in the South Pacific.

In March, the Sultan of Oman, and later Queen Beatrix of the Netherlands, visited Britain.

Colour is no longer an indication of national origin. Until this century most racial and religious groups remained concentrated in their homelands but today almost every country of the Commonwealth has become multi-racial and multi-religious. This change has not been without its difficulties, but I believe that for those with a sense of tolerance the arrival and proximity of different races and religions have provided a much better chance for each to appreciate the value of the others.

Extract from The Queen's Christmas Message

BELOW *Four generations, spanning the century, after the christening of Prince William at Buckingham Palace.*

A YEAR ON THE ROAD

The Queen and Prince Philip spent a good deal of the year 'on the road', taking in the Caribbean, Central and North America, Scandinavia, Africa and the Indian subcontinent. The journey began in Jamaica, and from there the royal party moved on to the west coast of the United States, visiting Hollywood, and then President and Mrs Reagan on the President's ranch in California. The American media reacted with coverage that was by no means uncritical; the love–hate relationship that America has with the British monarchy was again apparent. Unusually, for that part of the world, it rained a good deal.

Later in the year the friendship between the Palace and the White House, and between 10 Downing Street and the White House, was put under some strain. At issue was the invasion by America of Grenada, a small Caribbean island of which the Queen was head of state – a detail which seemed not to have registered with the President, although he was soon informed in no uncertain terms by, among others, Mrs Thatcher. Following an uprising in Grenada, and the overthrow and eventual murder of the Prime Minister, America claimed it had perceived a Cuban-backed threat to their security. But there was, to put it mildly, indignation in the Palace.

RIGHT *The American invasion of Grenada seemed to have been forgiven and forgotten when the Queen spoke at a state banquet in the White House.*

This 'mini war' took place in October, by which time the Queen and Prince Philip had been to Mexico, Canada and Sweden and were preparing to visit Bangladesh and India by way of Kenya. The culmination of the tour was the Commonwealth Heads of Government Conference in New Delhi, where the Queen also met Mother Teresa of Calcutta and presented her with the insignia of the Order of Merit. There was no doubting the Queen's continuing commitment to the Commonwealth – an enthusiasm which was not shared by Mrs Thatcher.

While in India the Queen's advisors planning the 1983 Christmas broadcast had filmed a sequence with the Queen in conversation with the Indian Prime Minister, Mrs Gandhi – an innovation which many thought did not succeed.

Austrailia was delighted to receive a visit from the Prince and Princess of Wales, particularly as they took the baby, Prince William, with them. The Waleses then went on to New Zealand where great crowds again turned out to see them.

1984

THE BRIGHTON BOMBING

The Queen was on a private visit to the United States at the time of the Brighton bombing. Horrified, she telephoned the Prime Minister and others to express her condolences and concern.

Mrs Thatcher survived the IRA's attempt to murder her and other members of the government when a bomb wrecked the Grand Hotel in Brighton where she and senior party leaders were staying during the Conservative party conference in October. Five people were killed and some 30 injured, many seriously. The bathroom Mrs Thatcher had been in just two minutes before the explosion was badly damaged when four floors disappeared from the centre of the hotel. Two of those who lost their lives were the MP Sir Anthony Berry and the wife of the Cabinet Minister John Wakeham. The wife of another Cabinet Minister, Norman Tebbitt, was badly injured.

On her return to London the Queen acted host to President Mitterand of France. This was not a routine state visit; strong Anglo–French relations were seen as a vital part of the United Kingdom's never entirely unambiguous attitude towards Europe, and the Queen had her part to play.

RIGHT *Forty years on, D-Day veterans march past the Queen and Prince Philip at Arromanches, on the battle sites in Normandy.*

The Queen and Prince Philip became grandparents for the fourth time when the Princess of Wales gave birth to Harry Charles Albert David who would be third in line of succession to the throne. The Prince and Princess had been married for three years.

The birth provided a diversion from some of the problems in the country, principally the strike by members of the National Union of Mineworkers, led by Arthur Scargill, which began in March. This bitter and violent dispute at times divided whole mining communities, even families. The Prime Minister was implacable, and when the law became involved the High Court ruled the strike to be illegal. Both the union and Mr Scargill were fined, union funds were sequestrated, and the Labour leader, Neil Kinnock, found himself having to tell the union to obey the law. The strike nevertheless continued for a full year until March 1985, but there was no doubt that the winner was Mrs Thatcher. The cost of the affair in human terms – which much upset and concerned the Queen – was immense.

An important and diplomatically sensitive state visit was paid by the Queen and Prince Philip to Jordan in March. King Hussein had long been a personal friend of the royal couple but it was crucial to British interests that there were good relations at national level between the two countries.

En route to Jordan, the Queen and Prince Philip spent a night privately in Cyprus. Later in the year they spent two weeks in Canada.

Prince Andrew was promoted to Lieutenant in February, and posted to HMS *Brazen*. While the ship was stationed in the South Atlantic the Prince revisited the Falkland Islands and opened a new airport there.

Prince Edward, meanwhile, having spent some time in New Zealand, was at Jesus College, Cambridge where, as well as reading history, he was developing an interest in drama.

Princess Anne carried out several hundred engagements during the year, and travelled abroad frequently, often on behalf of the Save the Children Fund, of which she was (and is) President.

One of the Prince of Wales's contributions to the year's enjoyment came in May when, in a speech at the Royal Institute of British Architects' 150th anniversary dinner, he referred to a planned extension to the National Gallery in Trafalgar Square as a 'monstrous carbuncle'.

OPPOSITE *The Thames barrier, designed to prevent London from serious flooding, was inaugurated by the Queen in May.*

ABOVE *Old friends meet again. The Queen and Prince Philip with King Hussein and Queen Noor during their visit to Jordan.*

One of the more encouraging developments since the war has been the birth of the Commonwealth. Like a child, it has grown, matured and strengthened, until today the vision of its future is one of increasing understanding and co-operation between its members. Notwithstanding the strains and stresses of nationalism, different cultures and religions and its growing membership, the Commonwealth family has still managed to hold together and to make a real contribution to the prevention of violence and discord.

Extract from The Queen's Christmas Message

SARAH FERGUSON CAPTURES THE HEADLINES

KEY EVENTS

Mikhail Gorbachev, described by Mrs Thatcher as 'a man we can do business with', assumed supreme control in the USSR.

•••

A state of emergency was imposed in many parts of South Africa.

•••

In Britain, 56 people died at Bradford City football stadium in May when a fire destroyed an old wooden stand in minutes. The same month violence from British fans led to a wall collapsing at the Heysel stadium in Belgium; 41 Italian and Belgian fans were killed, and a further 400 injured, before the European Cup Final between Juventus of Turin and Liverpool.

•••

In Britain the year-long miners' strike ended in defeat for the National Union of Mineworkers.

•••

The Synod of the Church of England approved the ordination of women.

•••

Orson Welles, Yul Brunner and Rock Hudson died. So too did the British poet and novelist Robert Graves, and fabric designer Laura Ashley.

For the Queen and Prince Philip the annual summer break at Balmoral was immediately followed by a month-long tour of the Caribbean. Making their first visit to Belize, the couple received an enthusiastic welcome, though when a local delicacy, Gibnut, was served at the state banquet Western headline writers had a field day: 'Queen Eats Rat!'

In the Bahamas the Queen again carried out her duties as head of the Commonwealth when she attended the Heads of Government meeting in Nassau. South Africa dominated the agenda, with Mrs Thatcher holding out against sanctions. With her customary aplomb the Queen studiously avoided any impression of taking the British official line against that of other Commonwealth members.

The tour had its lighter moments. The presidents and prime ministers had been invited to dine with the Queen on the royal yacht which had docked in the port at Nassau. In order to avoid anti-government demonstrations in the town, the Prime Minister of the Bahamas arranged for them to be taken round to *Britannia* by launch. They did indeed avoid a political storm but ran into a meteorological one, during which their launch hit a sand bank. When they finally arrived some were not at all keen to face food, even if it was cooked by the Queen's chef!

In June another significant event was the introduction of Sarah Ferguson into the royal family. Through the Princess of Wales she had been invited to join the

OPPOSITE Prince Andrew and Sarah Ferguson became an 'item' during the year after she had been invited to be a guest at the Queen's Ascot week house-party.

RIGHT The Prince and Princess of Wales drew huge crowds whenever and wherever they appeared together on engagements throughout the country.

Queen's Ascot Week house party at Windsor, and at lunch she was seated next to Prince Andrew. Sarah, like her father, Major Ronald Ferguson who was the Prince of Wales's polo manager, was already known to the family, but this occasion was the start of a much closer relationship.

For some time images of the terrible famines in Africa, and particularly Ethiopia, had been appearing on the television screens of the more affluent countries. Irish rock star Bob Geldof, with vision, enterprise and sheer bloody mindedness, was determined to help. He followed up his 1984 rock concert, Band Aid, in aid of Ethiopia's starving, with an even more impressive enterprise – Live Aid. The Prince and Princess of Wales joined Geldof at Wembley for the concert which attracted the world's leading rock artists, an audience of somewhere near one and a half billion, and contributions of an estimated $70 million.

The Queen and Prince Philip also made a state visit to Portugal, 'Britain's oldest ally', where their host was President Antonio Eanes. Incoming state visitors were Dr Hastings Banda, President of Malawi, President de la Madrid of Mexico and the Amir of Qatar.

BELOW *The Amir of Qatar is welcomed by the Queen and Prince Philip at the Grand Entrance to Buckingham Palace.*

1986

ROYAL WEDDING II

RIGHT *The Queen reviews an amazing march past – the terracotta army in the tomb of China's Emperor Qin Shi Huang (circa 221 BC).*

*T*his was a year in which so much happened to the Queen – in Buckingham Palace and in Whitehall, in the UK and in China, as head of state and as head of the Commonwealth – that it seemed there was never less than a royal story a day. Other news also had an impact on the royal family.

Meanwhile, Mrs Thatcher was continuing her premiership, riding out such crises as the 'Westland affair', which led to the resignation of two of her cabinet (Michael Heseltine and Leon Britten), privatising British Gas, and backing Rupert Murdoch in his battle with the print unions.

Murdoch was – and remains – a republican (he is now an American citizen though born an Australian), and with Andrew Neil as editor, his *Sunday Times* was occasionally to prove a thorn in the monarchy's side. The Sunday before the wedding of Prince Andrew to Sarah Ferguson the paper published a front-page story claiming that the Queen was unhappy with Mrs Thatcher's policies, believing them to be uncaring, confrontational and divisive. The basis for these claims was said to be information from sources close to the Queen. In a letter to *The Times* (sister paper of *The Sunday Times*), the Queen's Private Secretary, Sir William Heseltine, responded, saying that this 'constitutes a totally unjustified slur on the impartiality and discretion of senior members of the Royal Household'.

Both Buckingham Palace and Downing Street were displeased by the story, which most people seemed to accept had at least a grain of truth in it. The Queen was certainly keener on the Commonwealth and its role than her Prime Minister – a fact which had long been established – but the principle of how a constitutional

monarch operates was now firmly reiterated: he or she acts on the advice of his or her Prime Minister and the Government of the day. The rumpus rumbled on for a while, with the Queen's Press Secretary, Michael Shea, suggested as being the 'source' – if there was one.

Apart from this the Queen had much to occupy her attention within her family. First there was her own 60th birthday, which was celebrated with a service of Thanksgiving in St George's Chapel, Windsor, followed by appearances on the Buckingham Palace balcony and the delivery by hundreds of children of thousands of daffodils.

A Birthday Gala at the Royal Opera House, Covent Garden, brought together such talents as Jessie Norman, Placido Domingo, the London Community Gospel Choir, Sir George Solti and many fine musicians, singers and dancers in a celebration presented by Dame Judi Dench and Paul Eddington. Despite bad weather thousands watched the performances on television screens in the piazza.

Three days later the Duchess of Windsor, now 90, died in her home in Paris. Her body was brought to Windsor where, after a service in St George's Chapel attended by 16 members of the royal family, she was buried alongside her husband at Frogmore.

In July the second royal wedding of the eighties provided another worldwide television spectacular. Prince Andrew and Sarah Ferguson had become engaged earlier in the year and Sarah was welcomed as another 'breath of fresh air' into the royal family. The Prince had been created Duke of York on the morning of his marriage, so it was as the Duke and Duchess of York that the couple emerged from Westminster Abbey.

King Juan Carlos of Spain paid a visit to the Queen in April. With the monarchy restored and democracy becoming established in Spain once more, it was a visit of great significance – the first to Britain by a Spanish monarch for 82 years. Earlier in the year the Queen and Prince Philip had been in Australia and New Zealand. In Australia the Queen signed the Australia Act, formally severing Australia's constitutional ties with the Government in London, while in New Zealand she ran into Maoris protesting at their treatment by her New Zealand Government. Eggs were thrown, although none struck the Queen, but this was an isolated incident in an overall enjoyable visit.

In October the Queen became the first British monarch to visit China, a diplomatically important tour that attracted huge crowds to see 'the English country female King', as the Chinese described her. The visit was a success, even though the abiding memory might well be of another of Prince Philip's gaffes. Chatting to a British student on an exchange scheme at Xian University, Prince Philip jokingly warned him that if he stayed too long he might get 'slitty eyes'. It gave the media all they needed: 'Philip Gets it Wrong'; 'the Great Wally of China' were just two headlines. The Chinese refused to be insulted and the tour continued on its triumphal way.

The royal yacht *Britannia* saw unexpected service when civil war broke out in South Yemen. On her way to Australia *Britannia* was diverted to Aden to rescue evacuees and over six days carried well over 1,000 to safety in Djibouti.

BELOW *Newly married and now the Duke and Duchess of York, the latest royal couple celebrate with the crowds gathered around Buckingham Palace.*

A Princess Royal

KEY EVENTS

In Britain, Mrs Thatcher led the Conservatives to a third general election victory.

• • •

Bob Hawke was re-elected Prime Minister in Australia, as was Charles Haughey in Ireland.

• • •

The car ferry The Herald of Free Enterprise *capsized off the Belgian port of Zeebrugge; 184 people died.*

• • •

Terry Waite, the Archbishop of Canterbury's special envoy to the Lebanon, was kidnapped by terrorists.

• • •

11 people were killed and some 60 others injured when an IRA bomb exploded in Enniskillen during a Remembrance Day parade.

• • •

In England, 14 people were killed and 15 wounded by a man on a shooting rampage in Hungerford; and 30 people died in a blaze at Kings Cross Underground Station in London. In October the 'storm of the century' caused deaths and much damage across southern England. Three days later Black Monday saw share values plummet worldwide.

• • •

The cellist Jacqueline Du Pré, actors Fred Astaire and Danny Kaye, and Rudolf Hess, former deputy to Adolf Hitler, died.

• • •

The jockey Lester Piggot was sent to prison for three years for tax evasion.

In June the Queen awarded Princess Anne the title of Princess Royal. This is the highest honour that a female member of the family can hold, below that of sovereign, and was in recognition of the Princess's 'devotion to duty and to public service'. The public recognised the honour as well justified. Not only was she President of the Save the Children Fund and of Riding for the Disabled, and Commandant-in-Chief of the WRNS, but the Princess had also succeeded her father as President of the International Equestrian Federation, was President of the British Olympics Association, and undertook many other duties.

Prince Edward also got himself into the headlines during the year. In January he resigned his commission in the Royal Marines, a move which led some to criticise him for being 'soft'; given that his father was Captain-General of the Royal Marines, others thought it a brave decision. Prince Edward's real passion, as was to become apparent, was for the theatre and for television. A foretaste of this came

RIGHT *The newly honoured Princess Royal arrives for one of the many engagements she carries out each year – formally, as here, or often totally informally overseas on behalf of the Save the Children Fund.*

OPPOSITE *The year's Christmas card showed the Queen and Prince Philip with their grandchildren, Prince William, Prince Harry and Peter and Zara Phillips.*

later in the year when the Prince organised 'It's a Royal Knock-out' – a television programme in which many younger members of the royal family took part. This raised some £1 million for charity but appalled many viewers and did very little for the dignity of the royal family.

In October another meeting of the Commonwealth Heads of Government took the Queen and Prince Philip to Canada. There were no other official or state visits abroad but the Queen was host to both King Fahd of Saudi Arabia and King Hassan II of Morocco when they came to Britain.

Now in her 87th year, the Queen Mother was in remarkably good health and in June attended the Queen's official birthday parade, Trooping the Colour, with the Princess of Wales and her great-grandson Prince William.

1988

AUSTRALIA CELEBRATES

KEY EVENTS

Three days before Christmas a bomb in a Boeing 747 en route from Frankfurt to New York exploded over the small Scottish town of Lockerbie. All 259 people on board and 11 more on the ground, were killed.

•••

In America, Vice-President George Bush won the November presidential election; President Mitterand of France was re-elected for a 2nd term; Benazir Bhutto became Prime Minister of Pakistan; General Pinochet was voted out of office in Chile; and PLO leader Yasser Arafat formally recognised the State of Israel.

•••

There were 166 deaths when the Piper Alpha oil rig caught fire in the North Sea.

•••

Three IRA terrorists were shot dead by British military personnel in Gibraltar.

•••

Millions of people were left homeless after devastating floods in Bangladesh.

•••

A rush hour train crash near Clapham Junction on the outskirts of London killed 36.

*T*he Queen and Prince Philip and the Prince and Princess of Wales all visited Australia – though at different times – to join in the bicentenary celebrations commemorating the arrival of the first Europeans in 1788. The Australians certainly showed they knew how to throw a good party and all the royals were caught up in the spirit of the year.

There was already strong speculation that all was not well between the Prince and Princess of Wales. Only seven years after their marriage, they were living increasingly separate lives and increasingly seen to be doing so.

The Prince and Princess were in Sydney on January 26 for the climax of the celebrations when a replica flotilla of ships carrying 'convicts' sailed into the

RIGHT *The Queen with Mohamed Al Fayed at Smith Lawn, Windsor.*

ABOVE *The Queen was in Australia to join in the national celebrations marking the arrival of the first Europeans in 1788.*

harbour, as Australia's first settlers to the colony had done 200 years earlier. Later in the year the Queen and Prince Philip spent three weeks in Australia, and the Queen opened the Expo 88 Exhibition in Brisbane.

The Sun newspaper paid £100,000 to charity after illegally publishing a private photograph belonging to the Queen, showing her with the baby Princess Beatrice.

It was a year of tragic events, of which the Lockerbie airline disaster just before Christmas was perhaps the most shocking – to people in both Britain and the United States. For the royal family there was personal sorrow when Hugh Lindsay, skiing with the Prince of Wales, was swept to his death in an alpine avalanche. He was a former equerry to the Queen and his wife was working in the Palace Press Office at the time of the accident. The Prince and the others in the party, including the Princess of Wales and the Duchess of York, were fortunate to escape with their lives.

Politically the world seemed somewhat more at peace. President Reagan, in his last year in office, met President Gorbachev in Moscow and genuine progress was made towards a strategic arms agreement. During a private visit to London the President and Mrs Reagan lunched with the Queen at Buckingham Palace.

Each Maundy Thursday, the day before Good Friday, the Queen visits a cathedral or church to distribute Maundy Money (specially minted silver coins) to the same number of men and women as her age. This year 62 men and 62 women received coins after the service held in Lichfield Cathedral. The tradition has its origins in the act of Christ when, in humility, he washed the feet of his disciples before the last supper and then commanded – mandated – them to 'love one another'. Commemorating this act is believed to have started in England in AD600.

THE COLLAPSE OF COMMUNISM

*T*he Queen, far better informed than most, nevertheless followed events in eastern Europe with increasing incredulity as one after another the seemingly permanent Communist regimes of the Warsaw Pact countries foundered in the face of popular protests through the summer and autumn: Poland, Bulgaria, Hungary, East Germany, Czechoslovakia, Rumania (after bloodshed and the execution by firing squad of the Ceausecus). Then in November the world watched as the Berlin Wall was broken down and families and friends from East and West were reunited, in some cases for the first time since 1961. It was the most potent symbol of dramatic change.

Gorbachev had been a guest of the Queen at Windsor Castle in April. At any time such a visit would have been interesting, but Mr Gorbachev was himself to come under pressure to bring democracy to the Soviet Union and the conversation must have been fascinating. During the meeting it was agreed that the Queen would visit Russia, although no date was fixed at the time.

Early in the year the Queen and Prince Philip had attended the celebrations to mark the 350th anniversary of the establishment of a parliament on the island of Barbados. As head of state the Queen took a full part in the proceedings in

RIGHT A day of warm sunshine and warm welcome as the Queen visits Jersey in the Channel Islands.

OPPOSITE *The Queen with Mr Gorbachev during his visit to Britain.*

BELOW *One of the last photographs taken of the Princess Royal and Captain Mark Phillips together, before they announced they were to separate. They were at their home, Gatcombe Park.*

Bridgetown. The system set up in 1639 had certainly served this peaceful and generally stable Caribbean kingdom well.

In Kuala Lumpur in October the Queen was once once more present at a Commonwealth Heads of Government meeting. South Africa was again very much on the agenda. Were sanctions working? Were there signs of progress towards the ending of apartheid? The Queen, as ever, heard all shades of opinion expressed. The Queen and Prince Philip had spent time in Singapore before the conference, where the President was now Wee Kim Wee.

President Ibrahim Babangida of Nigeria had met the Queen in London when he paid a state visit in May. The head of state of the United Arab Emirate, Sheikh Zayed bin Sultan al-Nahayan, was the Queen's guest in July.

In 1998 the Prince of Wales had written and presented a television programme, 'A Vision of Britain', and a book based on the programme was published in September. In it the Prince set out his views on conservation and stressed the necessity as he saw it for architects to design buildings with the needs of the people who would use them in mind. These were two themes to which he was to refer regularly in the years ahead.

The sad but by then inevitable decision of the Princess Royal and Captain Mark Phillips to separate came at the end of August. The royal family were, as usual, at Balmoral, where the Queen was a much needed 'granny' to Peter and Zara Phillips.

If we can reduce selfishness and jealousy, dishonesty and injustice, the nineties can become a time of peace and tranquillity for children and grown ups, and a time for working together for the benefit of our planet as a whole.

Extract from The Queen's Christmas Message

1990

In South Africa Nelson Mandela's release from prison came after 27 years of incarceration. As Deputy President of the African National Congress (ANC), he began negotiations that were to end white rule and the policy of apartheid.

•••

In the USSR Mikhail Gorbachev was formally elected Executive President of the Soviet Union, was awarded the Nobel Peace Prize, and had a fruitful summit meeting with President Bush in Washington.

•••

Lech Walesa, the leader of the Polish trade union Solidarity, was elected President of Poland following the dissolution of the Polish Communist party.

•••

East Germany and the German Federal Republic unified on October 3.

•••

In August Iraqi troops invaded the neighbouring oil-producing kingdom of Kuwait. The United Nations issued demands for an immediate withdrawal and the imposition of punitive sanctions.

•••

At home Mrs Thatcher lost the leadership of the Conservative party to John Major and stood down as Prime Minister after 11 years in office.

•••

Greta Garbo, Leonard Bernstein, Sammy Davies Jnr and the great cricketer, Sir Len Hutton, died.

NOW THE NINETIES

The 1890s became known as the 'Naughty Nineties', with the then Prince of Wales, later King Edward VII, doing his bit to justify the description. For the Queen and her family the nineties of the 20th century were at times really quite nasty, with 1992 described vividly by the Queen as her 'annus horribilis'.

The decade began with money on the royal agenda. The Civil List had once again been under review and Parliament recognised that much had been done in the Palace to keep costs down. In July it was announced that for the next ten years a set annual allocation would be made to the Civil List. This would be more than was required in the earlier years, allowing a reserve to be built up to take into account inflation in the second half of the decade. From this, the Queen was to receive (not as pay but to meet the expenses involved as head of state) £7.9 million a year; the Queen Mother £643,000 a year; and Prince Philip £359,000. As ever, there was wide speculation about the Queen's private wealth. The Palace gave no details but again pointed out that many of the assets technically owned by the Queen – the Crown jewels and the royal collection, for example – were not 'disposable' but part of the national heritage.

In February the Queen and Prince Philip were in New Zealand to attend the Commonwealth Games in Auckland and to join in the celebrations marking the 150th Anniversary of the Treaty of Waitangi (under which the Maori chiefs had ceded sovereignty to Queen Victoria). In June they made a state visit to Iceland before going on to Canada.

ABOVE *Now it is 90 not out! The Queen Mother celebrates her birthday with her daughters, grandchildren and great-grandchildren, outside Clarence House.*

OPPOSITE *Another grandchild, another christening. The Queen with the Duke and Duchess of York and their second daughter, Princess Eugenie.*

At home the Prince of Wales broke his right arm when he fell during a polo match. It was a bad fall, resulting in a severe fracture and the cancellation of official duties for some weeks. In March Prince Charles wrote and presented 'The Earth in Balance', a television programme that set out to spotlight global issues. His concern for the environment took him around the world; one visit in 1990 was to the rain forests of the Cameroons. He also continued to promote organic farming on his own estate at Highgrove, with the aim of reaching full organic status on the Home Farm by 1996.

The Princess of Wales was developing her own public life, devoting much time to charities helping children and the disabled, and working on behalf of Aids victims. Increasingly she and her husband were leading separate lives.

The Duke and Duchess of York celebrated the birth of Princess Eugenie on March 23.

CONFLICT IN THE GULF

KEY EVENTS

In the Gulf, after a month of relentless air attacks on Iraq and Iraqi forces, the Allied armies liberated Kuwait. The Allies lost 250 men, and Iraq a probable tens of thousands; 16 British troops were killed – 9 by 'friendly fire'.

•••

In the USSR President Gorbachev resigned, and by the end of the year the Soviet Union had become a commonwealth of republics (excluding the Baltic states), with Russia, led by Boris Yeltsin, the largest and most powerful.

•••

In the Balkans, Slovenia and Croatia declared their independence from Yugoslavia, which led to the start of yet another violent conflict. Albania too was in turmoil.

•••

In the Middle East the hostages John McCarthy (kidnapped in 1986), and Terry Waite (kidnapped 1987) were released.

•••

Rajiv Gandhi, a former Prime Minister of India (grandson of Nehru and son of Indira Gandhi), was assassinated.

•••

In November the publisher and newspaper owner Robert Maxwell was found drowned near his yacht in the Canary Islands.

•••

Margot Fonteyn, Martha Graham, Graham Greene, and Freddie Mercury of 'Queen', died.

*T*he early months of a turbulent year were dominated by operation Desert Storm against Iraq. This time the conflict did not directly involve members of the royal family. Prince Andrew was still in the Royal Navy but, unlike during the Falklands war, did not see action.

There was criticism from some sections of the media that some of the younger members of the royal family seemed altogether unconcerned by events in the Gulf. The Queen was sensitive to this and initiated a series of royal visits to military bases and to service families at home and abroad as the conflict continued. These visits were appreciated but there was nevertheless some feeling that the royal involvement was too little too late.

Success for the allies in the Gulf seemed to restore goodwill and in May, in part to mark the victory and to consolidate the Anglo–US 'special relationship', the Queen and Prince Philip visited President and Mrs Bush in the United States. The Queen became the first British monarch to address a joint meeting of Congress and she conferred an honorary knighthood on General Schwarzkopf ('Stormin' Norman'), the charismatic Allied Commander of the UN troops against Iraq.

The visit was memorable, too, for the 'talking hat'. At the ceremonial welcome

RIGHT *The Queen with General Norman Schwarzkopf and his wife after conferring an honorary knighthood on the American hero of the Gulf War.*

ABOVE *A very large rostrum all but obscures the Queen as she speaks on her arrival in Washington to visit President and Mrs Bush. The rostrum had been set for the President.*

Next February will see the Fortieth Anniversary of my father's death and of my Accession. Over the years I have tried to follow my father's example and to serve you as best I can. You have given me, in return, your loyalty and your understanding, and for that I give you my heartfelt thanks. I feel the same obligation to you that I felt in 1952. With your prayers, and your help, and with the love and support of my family, I shall try to serve you in the years to come.

Extract from The Queen's Christmas Message

in Washington the podium from which the speeches were to be made had been set up for the President rather than for the Queen, who is considerably shorter than President Bush. As a result, the Queen virtually disappeared when she spoke. She took it in good part and it gave her a good opening line when she spoke on Capitol Hill: 'I hope on this occasion that at least you can all see me.'

While in the United States the Queen and Prince Philip took the opportunity to help promote British film and television when they visited a BAFTA exhibition and attended a special lunch in the Library of Congress in Washington, DC.

Prince Philip celebrated his 70th birthday, and as the Queen moved towards the 40th anniversary of her succession some newspapers wondered if she would abdicate. That she would not, was made clear in her Christmas message.

The marriage of the Prince and Princess of Wales also continued to be the subject of speculation, some of it pretty close to the mark.

Overseas visits were paid to Namibia and Zimbabwe (now under the autocratic control of President Mugabe), which also involved a stopover in Nairobi, Kenya. President Lech Walesa of Poland was a guest of the Queen, and welcomed as a heroic and gracious man, a brave opponent of Communist tyranny; and in July President Mubarek of Egypt came to London – the first Egyptian head of state to pay such a visit since before the Suez crisis 35 years earlier.

A reign ended in January with the death of King Olav of Norway, a staunch friend of the Queen and of Britain.

ABOVE *The Queen arrives at Claridges Hotel in London for a banquet given by President Walesa of Poland during his state visit to Britain.*

1992

'ANNUS HORRIBILIS'

An inevitable headline for 1992, given the dramatic and emotional way in which the phrase was used by the Queen. She was speaking in November at a lunch in Guildhall, held to mark the 40th anniversary of her accession, just three days after she had watched with horror as parts of her childhood home, Windsor Castle, were destroyed by a ferocious fire. Her voice was hoarse with a cold and the after-effects of the smoke. '1992,' she said, 'is not a year on which I shall look back with undiluted pleasure. In the words of one of my more sympathetic correspondents, it has turned out to be an annus horribilis.' In the same speech she referred to the prevailing attitude of much of the media when she said: 'No institution, city, monarchy, whatever, should expect to be free from the scrutiny of those who give it loyalty and support, not to mention those who do not.'

Apart from the fire (the damage could be and was repaired), the Duke and Duchess of York had announced that they were to separate; the Princess Royal and Captain Mark Phillips had started divorce proceedings; and *Diana, Her True Story*, written by Andrew Morton, was published after being serialised in the Murdoch-owned *Sunday Times*. Though challenged and even derided at the time, it contained much that was to prove to be true.

These stark facts stood against a background of intrusive media speculation and of vivid images that had been reproduced around the world: the Duchess of York topless by a pool having her toes sucked by her 'financial adviser', John Bryan; the Princess of Wales alone in front of the Taj Mahal during a visit to India; the Prince and Princess of Wales together, looking deeply unhappy – these were among the most telling. It was not an easy time to project a role-model royal family.

And of course the Queen knew that more was to come. On December 9 the Prime Minister announced in the House of Commons that the Prince and Princess of Wales were to separate. There were, it was said, no plans for divorce and both

RIGHT *The Prince and Princess of Wales spent four days in South Korea in November. A month later it was announced they were to separate.*

149

ABOVE *The Queen
could only watch in
sorrow as parts of her
much-loved Windsor
Castle were destroyed
by fire as the horrible
year continued.*

parents would continue to be closely involved in bringing up Prince William and Prince Harry, who would also have the support of their grandparents, the Queen and Prince Philip.

At least the year ended with something for the family to celebrate. The Princess Royal, now divorced, married Commander Tim Laurence in the small Church of Scotland church at Crathie near Balmoral. It was a setting very different from that of Westminster Abbey 19 years earlier, and it marked a distinct change in moral attitudes. Not so very long before, another close member of the royal family, Princess Margaret, had decided not to marry the divorced man whom she loved.

At the Queen's request there were no great public celebrations to mark her 40 years on the throne. On the anniversary itself, in February, she had gone early to church at Sandringham and had then visited cancer patients at a nearby hospital. The BBC marked the year with a television documentary, 'Elizabeth R', produced by Edward Mirzeoff. It was in a way a sequel to 'Royal Family' but concentrated more on the Queen herself and the life she led. Shot over the course of a year, it revealed considerably more of the 'real' Queen than is often the case – not least her sense of humour.

Germany continued along the road of reunification, though at tremendous cost to the former West Germany. The Queen and Prince Philip paid a state visit to the newly united country in October. Their itinerary included Dresden, the city which had been virtually obliterated by RAF bombs during the Second World War; memories ran deep and an anti-British demonstration was staged while the Queen was there.

Earlier, in June, and as part of the United Kingdom's 'charm offensive' in Europe, the Queen and Prince Philip were in France as guests of President François Mitterand.

They also visited Malta in May, recalling the time they had spent there together during the early days of their marriage, when Prince Philip had been in command of his own ship.

1993

Having defeated President Bush in the presidential elections, Bill Clinton became the 42nd President of the United States.

•••

Peace of a kind broke out in the Middle East when Israel and the PLO agreed to recognise each other.

•••

Two South African leaders stood side by side as they shared the Nobel Peace Prize: President de Klerk and Nelson Mandela.

•••

In Pakistan Benazir Bhutto became Prime Minister for the second time.

•••

Despite more IRA violence and attacks on mainland Britain, including bombing a crowded shopping centre in Warrington, a peace agreement was signed before Christmas by John Major and Albert Reynolds, the Irish Prime Minister.

•••

King Baudouin of the Belgians died. Sir Matt Busby, novelists William Golding and Anthony Burgess, and the dancer Rudolf Nureyev also died. Everyone was horrified when two-year-old James Bulger was taken from a shopping mall by two ten-year-olds who beat and stoned him to death.

TAX RETURNS AT THE PALACE

*T*hat times do indeed change, even at Buckingham Palace, was borne out by two events. First, a 'Celebration of Europe' started the year off, with bonfires across the continent, as the European single market became a reality. What would that eventually come to mean for the United Kingdom?

Second, in February, the Prime Minister announced in the House of Commons that the Queen and the Prince of Wales would from now on pay tax on their private incomes. At the same time Civil List allowances for some members of the royal family would end. This had been under discussion for some years between Whitehall and the Palace, and detailed planning had lasted for several months. But there had been rumblings of discontent at the cost to the taxpayer of the royal family, and it seemed to many at the time that the announcement came in response to public pressure.

A change in Palace PR policy at this time allowed the Lord Chamberlain, Lord Airlie, to give a briefing to the media on the subject. It was a welcome move and it was the Lord Chamberlain again who, in April, was able to announce that the restoration of Windsor Castle would not depend on public money: Buckingham Palace would from now on open each summer to the public, and the proceeds from that would help to fund the restoration work. There would also be savings made from the monies set aside for the royal palaces, and visitors would be charged to visit the precincts of Windsor Castle. It was hoped the restoration work would be completed in time for the Queen and Prince Philip's golden wedding anniversary in November 1997.

Paul Keating, an avowed republican, became Australia's new Prime Minister, and considerations about Australia remaining a monarchy moved high up the agenda. Keating promised a referendum by the end of the century and appeared confident that Australia would be a republic by the year 2000.

A very special relationship came to an end when Margaret MacDonald (Bobo) died, aged 89. For nearly 70 years Bobo had served the Queen, first as nursemaid to the two princesses, then as the Queen's dresser; she had a unique place in the Queen's life.

The Queen celebrated the marriage of her nephew, Lord Lindley, the son of Princess Margaret and Lord Snowdon, to Serena Stanhope at a comparatively quiet and unostentatious wedding. Lord Lindley, a skilled furniture designer and manufacturer, had managed pretty successfully to grow up out of the limelight, as had his sister, Lady Sarah Armstrong-Jones.

LEFT *The Queen leaves the Queen's Chapel in St James's Palace after the funeral service of Margaret ('Bobo') MacDonald. She had been the Queen's dresser and close confidante throughout the reign.*

BELOW *Some of the first visitors to take the opportunity to tour the state apartments of Buckingham Palace, opened to the public for the first time in the summer, pass into the palace precincts.*

BELOW *Headlining the news of a development that had become inevitable and that came into effect in 1993.*

CIRCUS TALK
Valèrie Grove and the clown princess
Modern Times, page 14

TELEVISION
How the BBC will face a new century
Page 6

YACHTING
Leading solo sailor drowns
Page 40

INFOTECH ON FRIDAY Pages 34,35

THE TIMES

No. 64,501   FRIDAY NOVEMBER 27 1992   4

The Queen will pay income tax on her personal fortune

Howard signals £1,000 to council tax bills

BY NICHOLAS WOOD
POLITICAL CORRESPONDENT

Buckingham Palace
Summer Opening

Entrance
Ticket Holders Only

By Tunnel to France – and D-Day Remembered

KEY EVENTS

In Britain, the sudden death of the Labour leader, John Smith, resulted in the election of Tony Blair as leader of the party.

• • •

An IRA ceasefire was agreed at the end of August, with a 'complete cessation of military operations'. Loyalists in Ulster remained sceptical of the IRA's motives but talks began in Belfast between Sinn Fein and British government officials, and the ban on broadcasting for members of Sinn Fein (who had been allowed to appear on television but not to speak) was lifted.

• • •

Later in the year the Prime Minister of Ireland, Albert Reynolds, resigned.

• • •

The national lottery was launched with the first draw on November 19.

• • •

The first Anglican women priests were ordained, though not with the blessing of the whole church.

• • •

Former American President Richard Nixon died 20 years after resigning over the Watergate scandal. Two of Britain's playwrights, John Osborne and Dennis Potter, also died.

*D*escribed by the Queen as a mixture of French élan and British pragmatism, the Channel Tunnel linking the two countries was formally opened on May 6. President Mitterand met the Queen at Coquelles after she had opened the Eurostar Terminal at Waterloo and taken the train through the tunnel. Together they cut the red, white and blue ribbons, marking the realisation of a centuries-old – and very expensive – dream.

Another dream became a reality in South Africa when Nelson Mandela, leader of the African National Congress, was sworn in as President, the country's first black head of state. His call was for 'justice for all'. The ANC's success followed the first ever multi-racial elections in South Africa and owed much to the humility, wisdom and charisma of the new President. Later, the mutual respect and deep affection that the Queen and the President had for one another were to become clear to everyone. She was delighted when South Africa rejoined the Commonwealth.

A month after opening the Channel Tunnel the Queen, with Prince Philip, was back in France to commemorate the 50th anniversary of D-Day. On June 6 the Queen watched, visibly moved, as thousands of veterans paraded up the beach at

OPPOSITE *The Queen and President Mitterand of France cut the ribbon on May 6 and officially open the Channel Tunnel.*

ABOVE *An appropriate Christmas card to mark the 50th Anniversary of the D-Day Landings. The Queen and Prince Philip with survivors and veterans of the invasion of France in 1944.*

Arromanches where 50 years earlier, in the face of tremendous German fire power, they had come ashore to begin, in Normandy, the liberation of the whole of Europe. The Presidents of America and France and the Prime Minister of Canada were, of course, there too, Mitterand with his personal memories of the war in his homeland.

But the Queen still had family matters much on her mind. The annus horribilis was over but there was much unpleasantness to be faced, not least when, in a frank television interview with Jonathan Dimbleby, the Prince of Wales admitted his adultery with an unnamed woman. However, the name of Camilla

Parker Bowles was not, even then, a well kept secret. The purpose of the interview was to mark the 25th anniversary of Charles' investiture as Prince of Wales but that part of the programme became somewhat overlooked. A companion book was published; so too were others purporting to tell the 'truth' about the Prince of Wales.

The Prince of Wales caused the Queen concern of another kind while he was on a visit to Australia: an armed protester broke through a security cordon but was overpowered before he could do the Prince any harm. Princess Diana, meanwhile, was leading life as a 'single mother'; just about every aspect of it made the front pages.

In October, with Prince Philip, the Queen made a long-awaited state visit to Russia – 'a voyage of discovery' were her words. She was the first reigning British monarch to set foot on Russian soil. When Edward VII visited Tsar Nicholas II in 1908 they met only on their respective royal yachts anchored off Tallinn in the Baltic; the King never actually stepped ashore.

At home the royal family shared the general sorrow when the Labour leader John Smith died suddenly of a heart attack. In due course Tony Blair was elected his successor.

There was sadness in the royal family too when Jackie Onassis, the widow of President John Kennedy, died. Memories of the late President and of unveiling the John F. Kennedy memorial at Runnymede were revived.

Among other engagements at home, the Queen opened the new Jewel House in the Tower of London and, a delightful family occasion, attended the wedding of her niece, Lady Sarah Armstrong-Jones, who married Daniel Chatto. Both Princess Margaret's children had now flown the nest.

The Duchess of Kent converted to Roman Catholicism. She was received into the church by the Archbishop of Westminster, Cardinal Basil Hume, at a private ceremony.

LEFT *Yeomen of the Guard escort the Queen at the Tower of London where, in March, she opened the new Jewel House, designed to better display the Crown Jewels.*

FIFTY YEARS OF 'PEACE'

KEY EVENTS

Fighting continued in Eastern Europe, with Russian air and ground attacks against Grozny, capital of Chechnya, and NATO air strikes against Serbian forces in Bosnia. A ceasefire was brokered in the Balkans after President Clinton threatened to send in US ground forces to back the NATO raids.

• • •

Jacques Chirac was elected President of France. The Israeli Prime Minister, Yitzhak Rabin, was assassinated.

• • •

In the USA a truck loaded with explosives by a right-wing political activist, Timothy McVeigh, blew up a Federal building in Oklahoma city, killing 168 people. More than 5,000 people died and over 25,000 were injured by an earthquake in the Japanese city of Kobe.

• • •

O.J. Simpson was found 'not guilty' of murdering his wife and a male friend.

• • •

Two former Prime Ministers, Lord Wilson (Harold Wilson) and Lord Home (Sir Alec Douglas-Home), and Fred Perry died.

*T*he celebrations to mark the anniversary of, first, the end of the war in Europe in May 1945 and then, in August, the war with Japan, brought huge crowds into London and to Buckingham Palace. On both occasions the Queen with Queen Elizabeth the Queen Mother and Princess Margaret appeared on the Palace balcony as they had 50 years earlier – though at that time it had been with the King and the Prime Minister, Winston Churchill. Now they led the anniversary celebrations, singing along with Dame Vera Lynn. On VE night itself, in 1945, the two young Princesses had slipped out of the Palace (Princess Elizabeth in her ATS uniform) with some guardsmen friends, to join the crowd in the Mall calling for the King and Queen.

Of huge significance was the visit that the Queen and Prince Philip paid to South Africa in March – not least for personal reasons. Journalists covering the tour said that the Queen had seldom looked so spontaneously happy. There were three reasons for this: her admiration and liking for President Mandela; her delight that South Africa had rejoined the Commonwealth; and happy memories of her previous visit to the country in 1947. It was on that trip, with her parents and already in love, that she made her memorable (and first) 21st birthday broadcast, in which she dedicated her life 'to the peoples of the British Commonwealth and Empire'. On her return to London she and the then Lieutenant Philip Mountbatten RN became engaged. The 1995 visit was a total success.

Family matters were less happy. In November the Princess of Wales gave an interview to the BBC's Panorama. In it she admitted to a love affair with Major

RIGHT *Back in South Africa for the first time since 1947, the Queen, this time with Prince Philip, enormously enjoyed the hospitality and company of President Nelson Mandela.*

ABOVE *VE Day 1995. Fifty years after she had stood on the Palace balcony with King George VI and Winston Churchill to celebrate the end of the war in Europe, the Queen Mother takes centre stage. With the Queen and Princess Margaret she watches a fly-past of wartime aircraft. They also joined in with the crowds around the Palace as they sang 'We'll Meet Again'.*

RIGHT *In the famous home of the old transatlantic liners – Southampton – the Queen named the P&O's new cruise liner, the Oriana.*

ORIANA

P&O
ORIANA

ABOVE *Baroness Thatcher curtsies to the Queen at an evening reception. Lady Thatcher was the Queen's prime minister from 1979 until almost the end of 1990.*

James Hewitt, said that her marriage to the Prince had been 'crowded' (a reference to Camilla Parker Bowles), and wondered if her husband would ever become King. For herself she said she would like to be 'the queen of people's hearts'.

The interview, pre-recorded, was a secret that was kept from the Queen and the Palace until almost the last moment. Relations between Buckingham Palace and the BBC became somewhat strained as a result. Seldom before had anyone used television in such a calculated and ruthless way; it was compelling viewing but sad to watch.

One consequence was that the Queen took direct action. After talking to the Prime Minister and the Archbishop of Canterbury, as well as to other advisors, she wrote separately to her son and daughter-in-law, urging them to resolve the situation with an early divorce. The Queen no doubt had the welfare of her two grandsons very much in mind; clearly matters could not continue as they were. Overall, the country agreed.

Life of course had to go on, and the Queen received state visits from the Amir of Kuwait and President Ahtisaari of Finland. The visit of the Amir of Kuwait came in the wake of the Gulf war, and there were naturally expressions of gratitude to the United Kingdom for its part in reclaiming Kuwait from the Iraqis.

Elsewhere, Quebec voted to remain a province of Canada; President Clinton visited Northern Ireland; and the Prince of Wales became the first member of the royal family to pay an official visit to the Irish Republic since 1911 when he went to Dublin.

1996

Dunblane, Docklands and Divorce

A year of much sadness: the horror of the massacre at Dunblane; the end of the IRA's ceasefire with a bomb in London's docklands; and two royal divorces.

Despite the violence with which we have all become familiar on film and television, nothing could prepare people for what happened in a small Scottish town on March 13. The appalling and senseless shooting in the primary school at Dunblane shocked the world. Thomas Hamilton, known to be unstable, walked into the gymnasium of the school and shot dead a teacher and 16 children, wounding another teacher and five more children, before killing himself. There was no hiding the grief felt by the Queen and the Princess Royal when, four days after the shootings, they went to Dunblane to mourn the dead and comfort the families as best they could. It was, by chance, Mothering Sunday. The Prime Minister, John Major, and the Labour leader, Tony Blair, had also been to the town to express their own and the nation's grief.

As Queen of Australia, the Queen had further cause for distress when news came of another massacre, this time in Tasmania. A gunman, Martin Bryant, ran amok in Port Arthur, a resort near Hobart, killing 35 people, one of them a baby. He received 35 life sentences.

The two royal divorces were accepted by most people with sadness but resignation. The Prince and Princess of Wales ended their marriage in August; the Duke and Duchess of York divorced in April. There was much sympathy for their children, and for the Queen and Prince Philip as parents and grandparents. Three children married; three children divorced – the concept of the House of Windsor as a model family was over. The Princess of Wales, no longer eligible to be called Her Royal Highness, took the title Diana, Princess of Wales. She gave up many of

RIGHT *The Press Association newsflash which brought the news that the Prince and Princess of Wales were to start divorce proceedings.*

XXX AAA HHH
TAB8357 2 HHH 30 PA RUSH
1 ROYAL Divorce
PA NEWSFLASH: Prince and Princess of Wales will start divorce proceedings on Monday (July 15) and should end their 15-year marriage on August 28, lawyers announced today. (
mf mw
121530 JUL 96 (

I shall never forget the State visit of President Mandela. That most gracious of men has shown us all how to accept the facts of the past without bitterness, how to see new opportunities as more important than old disputes and how to look forward with courage and optimism. His example is a continuing inspiration to the whole Commonwealth and to all those everywhere who work for peace and reconciliation.

Extract from The Queen's Christmas Message

her charitable patronages and said she hoped the media would give up their round-the-clock watch on her every move. She must have known that this would fall on deaf ears.

Supported by her husband and by her mother, the Queen maintained her dignity throughout this family turmoil. She visited Poland and Czechoslovakia, the latter still a federation though soon to divide, and in July Nelson Mandela arrived to pay the first state visit by a president of South Africa. He received the warmest possible welcome, the Queen showing no outward sign of the sadness she must have been experiencing.

In Australia the future of the monarchy was very much a live issue as the republican movement gained strength. The Queen still had an approval rating there of 75%, far above the dreams of any politician, but the relevance of the existing constitution and its value to Australia as the 21st century drew near was being questioned more vigorously than it had since 1936 and the abdication crisis.

ABOVE *In Prague, on her visit to the Czech Republic in March, the Queen with her host, President Havel.*

1997

A WEEK WHEN THE WORLD SEEMED TO STOP

KEY EVENTS

Tony Blair became the youngest Prime Minister for 150 years when 'New Labour' won the general election with an overwhelming majority; 18 years of Conservative rule was over. John Major resigned as leader of the Conservative party and the Tories elected its youngest leader since Pitt the Younger, 36-year-old William Hague.

• • •

The new government announced referenda in Scotland and Wales to decide on new constitutions to bring them differing degrees of independence from Westminster.

• • •

In July the IRA announced another ceasefire. The peace process trundled on.

• • •

Dolly, a sheep cloned from a single cell of her mother, was presented to the world.

• • •

Mother Teresa, founder of the Order of Missionaries of Charity, died in Calcutta, and Deng Xiaoping, China's senior political figure, also died.

RIGHT *Diana, Princess of Wales, in London just a month before her tragic death. As she did so often, she was visiting a children's hospital.*

In the early hours of Sunday August 31 Diana, Princess of Wales and her then lover, Dodi Fayed, left the Ritz Hotel in Paris. The car in which they and a bodyguard were being driven crashed in an underpass in the centre of the city. Dodi Fayed and the driver were killed outright; it is believed that Diana was still alive when taken from the wreckage but she died soon afterwards in the Pitié Salpétrière Hospital. Her bodyguard, Trevor Rees-Jones, was very seriously injured. The driver, Henri Paul, was found to be over three times above the alcohol level allowed in France.

The Queen and Prince Philip, Prince Charles, Prince William and Prince Harry, with other members of the royal family, were at Balmoral and were to remain there for some days after the tragedy. Four hundred miles south, in London, tens of thousands of people gathered at Buckingham Palace and at the Princess's home, Kensington Palace, to lay floral tributes, bring toys and messages and to gain comfort from an extraordinary outpouring of shared grief and emotion

ABOVE *The Queen
leads the royal family
in paying their
respects to the
Princess as the cortege
passes Buckingham
Palace on its way to
Westminster Abbey.*

which few, if any, had ever experienced. Across the country and throughout the world the reaction was the same. Around Buckingham Palace, along the Mall, in Kensington Gardens and in the streets adjoining St James's Palace the public gathered to weep and to mourn in the days that followed. Of all ages and from all sections of the population, men, women and children were united in grief for the young woman whom Tony Blair described as 'the people's princess'.

Later on the Sunday, August 31, the Prince of Wales flew to Paris to bring the

body of his former wife back to London. The Queen and Prince Philip, grandparents now above all else, remained with William and Harry in Balmoral but by the middle of the week the royal family was facing criticism from both public and press for not returning to London at such a time, and for not flying a flag at half-mast on Buckingham Palace. There was genuine public bewilderment at what was perceived as a lack of emotional response, especially when contrasted with Diana's own spontaneity.

The Queen had felt that as the young Princes had been at Balmoral when their mother died it was best that the family should remain there to give them what comfort they could in the immediate aftermath. Notice was, however, taken of public feeling. First the Union flag was flown, half-mast, at the Palace, then the Duke of York and Prince Edward returned to London to walk among the crowds and see the tributes.

Prince Charles and his sons flew back from Scotland on the Friday, the day before the funeral and, movingly, mingled with the thousands around Kensington Palace. The Queen and Prince Philip themselves returned to Buckingham Palace that afternoon, and they too walked among the crowds surrounding the Queen Victoria Memorial. That evening, in a live television and radio broadcast from the

Palace, the Queen paid tribute to Diana, speaking of her own grief and of her responsibilities as a grandmother.

The funeral service in Westminster Abbey moved all who attended or watched or listened. It was estimated that over a million people lined the route as the coffin, mounted on a gun carriage, moved from the Chapel Royal opposite St James's Palace to the Abbey. It was followed on its final stages by the three Princes – Charles, William and Harry – by the Princess's brother, Earl Spencer, and by Prince Philip. The bearing of Diana's sons was mature beyond their years.

As the cortège passed Buckingham Palace the Queen led other members of the family out of the forecourt to pay their respects. In the Abbey the service included an oration by Earl Spencer in which he criticised the media for being intrusive and also, by implication, the attitude of the royal family towards his sister. A rewritten version of his song 'Candle in the Wind' was played and sung by Elton John. Afterwards, the coffin was driven, through more crowds and more floral tributes, to the Spencer's family home at Althorp in Northamptonshire.

Earlier in the year, in March, the Queen, encouraged by her husband, moved with the electronic times and launched the Buckingham Palace website. It proved an immediate success and as more and more homes came on line, received a huge number of 'hits'.

The same month brought an announcement of changes in the financing of royal travel. Instead of these costs being met from various government departments they would be controlled by the Palace out of an annual travel allowance of almost £20 million from the Exchequer. One charge that was no longer incurred after the end of the year was that of the royal yacht *Britannia*, which was decommissioned at Portsmouth after almost 44 years' service. The ceremony was attended by the Queen and by other members of her family, all of whom shared her affection for the ship. The decision not to replace *Britannia* met with much public criticism, although a 'leaner' monarchy was clearly appropriate to the times.

In June, accompanied by the new Labour Prime Minister, Tony Blair, the Prince of Wales flew to Hong Kong where, at midnight on June 30, the Union flag was lowered for the last time and one of Britain's last remaining colonies was returned to China after 99 years. The former Conservative party chairman and MP for Bath, Chris Patten, was the last Governor of the colony.

After the turmoil of the late summer, the autumn was a happier time for the Queen and Prince Philip. The restoration of Windsor Castle after the fire of 1992 was completed, ahead of schedule and on budget. Then came the celebrations to mark the royal couple's golden wedding. There were

BELOW *The Queen and the Queen Mother leave Westminster Abbey after the funeral service, when Earl Spencer gave the address and Sir Elton John sang a special tribute.*

telling speeches from both the Queen and Prince Philip. At a lunch in Guildhall, Prince Philip said that the essential ingredient of a happy marriage was tolerance: 'The Queen has the quality of tolerance in abundance,' he told the guests. He also paid tribute to their children and grandchildren. While the Queen, at a celebration dinner in the Whitehall Banqueting House, spoke of her wish to hear the message of the people and to be guided by it. She commented that what was relayed to the royal family from the public, 'obscured as it can be by deference, rhetoric or the conflicting currents of public opinion', was often harder to read than the message signalled to politicians by voters. But, she added, with events of the earier part of the year very much in mind, 'read it we must'.

In October the Queen and Prince Philip had visited Pakistan and India, visits which certainly generated some 'heat and dust'. It was not tigers this time – certainly not the shooting of them – but a remark of the Foreign Secretary, Robin Cook, who was with the royal party as is usual on such occasions. His comment that India and Pakistan should resolve their differences over the disputed territory of Kashmir provoked anger in India, and the Queen was inevitably involved by association in the row; she herself well knew how to avoid such diplomatic upsets.

ABOVE *The Queen goes online as, in March, she inaugurates the Buckingham Palace website. It was an instant hit.*

LEFT *An anniversary lunch at Guildhall in the City of London, as the Queen and Prince Philip celebrate 50 years of marriage.*

1998

THE GREAT WAR REMEMBERED

RIGHT *The Queen drops in at the Bridge Inn at Topsham, Devon, to meet the landlady and some of her regulars.*

The Queen and Prince Philip paid a poignant visit to France and Belgium to mark the 80th anniversary of the 1918 armistice. In a deeply moving ceremony at the Menin Gate in Ypres the Queen laid a wreath in memory of the fallen, and in Paris she unveiled a statue of Winston Churchill. Moving, too, was the dignity of the veterans, with their medals and their memories.

The heads of state of both principal wartime enemies paid state visits to London. Emperor Akihito of Japan came in May, to be met by demonstrations by former prisoners-of-war (as had his father, Hirohito, 29 years earlier); President Roman Herzog of Germany was the Queen's guest in December.

Other less formal occasions in the Queen's programme included a visit to the Bridge Inn at Topsham in Devon, a ride in a taxi to mark the use of liquid petroleum gas in four of the royal cars, and a trip to see the pantomime *Aladdin* in Harrogate, which brought back memories of the pantos she and her sister used to put on each year at Windsor Castle when they were children. She also inaugurated the restored Albert Memorial in Hyde Park, opposite the Royal Albert Hall.

In her Christmas message the Queen paid a warm tribute to her mother for the Queen Mother's outstanding service: 'She has an extraordinary capacity to bring happiness into other people's lives.' She also approved the introduction of

ABOVE *A tribute from France. A memorial statue of Sir Winston Churchill was unveiled in Paris by the Queen and President Chirac – appropriately, on November 11.*

sexual equality in the line of succession to the throne. For hundreds of years the rule of primogeniture had prevailed, in which male offspring took precedence over females. Now the firstborn, regardless of sex, would succeed.

Another major change, this one to the British constitution, was announced by the Queen in her speech at the Opening of Parliament in November. Hereditary peers would lose their automatic right to sit and to vote in the House of Lords; instead, for a transitional period, some would be elected by their fellow peers to sit with those who had been appointed life peers.

One peer, the Prince of Wales, was 50 on November 14. The celebrations included a party at Buckingham Palace during which the Queen, proposing the toast to her son, spoke movingly of the pride she and Prince Philip felt in the Prince's achievements, particularly through his Trust. Camilla Parker Bowles was not at the Palace but did attend the party Prince Charles held at his own home, Highgrove, in Gloucestershire. The photo of her driving in through the estate gates made just about every front page.

Princess Margaret suffered a stroke while on holiday in the Caribbean island of Mustique and was flown home to London. The Prince of Wales took his sons to Canada where both young Princes proved extremely popular, and William was a big hit with the thousands of teenage girls who turned out to see them.

Responding to the 'message' of the public, so clearly voiced at the time of the death of Princess Diana, the Union flag was now flown at Buckingham Palace whenever the Queen was away; the royal standard was raised as usual when she was in residence.

It is not always easy for those in their teens or twenties to believe that someone of my age – of the older generation – might have something useful to say to them. But I would say that my mother has much to say to me. Indeed, her vigour and enjoyment of life is a great example of how to close the so-called generation gap. She has an extraordinary capacity to bring happiness into other people's lives. And her own vitality and warmth is returned to her by those whom she meets.

Extract from The Queen's Christmas Message

BELOW *The Albert Memorial, splendidly restored to its original golden glory, was unveiled by the Queen – the Prince Consort's great-great granddaughter – in October. As the Victorians might have said, a pyrotechnic display followed.*

CONSTITUTIONAL CHANGES

KEY EVENTS

In Washington, President Clinton was cleared of 'high crimes and misdemeanours', and the Senate voted by 55 votes to 45 not to remove him from office.

•••

A plane piloted by John F. Kennedy Jnr crashed on America's East Coast, killing Kennedy, his wife and her sister. John-John, aged three, had touched everyone's heart when seen saluting his father's coffin at the President's funeral.

•••

Much of the world joined Jordanians in mourning the death of King Hussein.

•••

The Israeli Prime Minister, Benjamin Netanayahu, was voted out of office and Ehud Barak took over.

•••

On mainland Europe the euro went into circulation.

•••

In London, a train crash at Ladbroke Grove resulted in 27 deaths and many injuries.

•••

The immensely popular television presenter Jill Dando was shot dead outside her home in Fulham.

OPPOSITE *In Cardiff, the Queen leaves the National Assembly for Wales with the Presiding Officer, Lord Elis Thomas.*

RIGHT *The Queen with Donald Dewar, Scotland's first First Minister, after the opening of the new Parliament in Edinburgh in July.*

*T*o begin at the end: 31 December 1999, officially the last day of the 20th century, did not go entirely to plan in the United Kingdom.

Around the world, from the South Pacific and across all the time zones, the dawn of the 21st century was celebrated with fireworks, dance, music, worship and with hope.

In Britain the Millennium Dome was intended to be the focal point of the Government's celebrations. The Queen and Prince Philip travelled comfortably by barge down the Thames to join the Prime Minister and some 10,000 guests, but thanks to the maldistribution of tickets and confusion at entrances to the new Jubilee tube line, not all of these reached the party so effortlessly. Nevertheless, assisted by pupils from a nearby primary school, the Queen officially opened the Dome at a quarter of an hour before midnight. The new century was seen in with a kiss from her husband, the singing of 'Auld Lang Syne' as she linked hands with Prince Philip and the Prime Minister, and a glass of champagne. The Dome, as it was to transpire, was in for a difficult year.

The royal programme for the preceding 12 months had been an exceptionally busy one (the Queen was now 73), with major constitutional changes involving Wales and Scotland, and a boost from Australia, among the highlights. In May the Queen opened the Welsh National Assembly and attended a service in Llandaff Cathedral. Scotland was to have its own Parliament, and at the opening ceremony

On Saturday June 19 Prince Edward and Miss Sophie Rhys-Jones were married at St George's Chapel, Windsor. The comparatively informal occasion was in great contrast to the weddings of the Prince's two older brothers, and there was no military presence. Guests were even requested not to wear hats, although the Queen Mother did! On the day of their marriage the couple became the Earl and Countess of Wessex.

in Edinburgh in July the Queen of Scots restored an authority that had last been in existence 292 years before. On this historic occasion the Duke of Hamilton preceded the Queen into the Chamber, carrying the Scottish crown.

Elections in Wales for the new Assembly and in Scotland for the restored Parliament had taken place in May; in both cases Labour lost support. In Wales, as a result of Welsh nationalist Plaid Cymru successes, Labour formed a minority government, and in Scotland Labour shared control with the Liberal Democrats.

Results of the referendum on the future of the monarchy in Australia (where voting is compulsory) came through early in November, and showed that 54% of Australians wished to retain it. Republicans blamed their defeat on the alternative proposed: a president elected not by the people but by Members of Parliament. On the same day, in Cardiff, the Queen presented the Rugby World Cup to the winning Australian captain, John Eales, an avowed republican.

Other state business included visits by the Queen and Prince Philip to South Korea in April, where the Queen celebrated her birthday, and to Ghana, Mozambique and South Africa in November.

At home the royal programme was becoming decidedly less formal. In March the Queen and Prince Philip spent a day visiting the theatres of the West End, and in Scotland in July the Queen had tea with Susan McCarron at her home on a Glasgow housing estate. While the cameras were present conversation was stilted, but in private the Queen and Mrs McCarrow had a great chat.

Innovations included the public display of the royal art collection in a new

RIGHT *Young
members of the cast of
Oklahoma meet the
Queen after she had
enjoyed the musical at
London's Lyceum
Theatre. She and the
Duke spent a day in
the West End's
theatreland.*

LEFT *The statue of Eric
Morecambe, who died
after a heart attack in
1984, was unveiled on
the Promenade at
Morecambe by the
Queen. Eric Morecambe
and Ernie Wise were
two of the Queen's
favourite comedians.*

175

gallery in Buckingham Palace, and television cameras allowed into the Palace to cover investiture ceremonies. One of the first investitures to be seen on television news was that of the actress Julie Walters receiving her OBE.

The Queen presented Prince Charles's Prince's Trust with a royal charter; she had a good win at Ascot with her horse Blueprint (prize money £35,520); and she demoted a Palace footman found offering the royal corgis whisky and gin!

The health of Princess Margaret continued to cause concern following her stroke a year earlier. She had still not completely recovered when, in March, she was treated for severe burns after stepping into a bath of scalding water while on holiday in Mustique.

The Queen Mother carried on with her astonishingly active life and celebrated her 99th birthday on August 4.

At the beginning of December it became known that the Queen had chosen to buy her Christmas puddings from the Tesco supermarket, rather than, as she had done for many years, from Harrods. The order was for 1,411 – she gives many as Christmas gifts. Palace–Harrods relations were definitely strained by Mohamed Al Fayed's wild accusation that Prince Philip had been party to a plot to bring about the death of Diana, Princess of Wales.

In her Christmas message at the end of the century the Queen spoke of timeless values: 'The future is not only about new gadgets, modern technology or the latest fashion, important as they may be. At the centre of all our lives – today and tomorrow – must be the message of caring for others, the message at the heart of Christianity and of all the great religions.'

BELOW *'Auld Lang Syne' at the Millennium Dome as midnight strikes and hands are joined. The Prime Minister is on the Queen's left.*

2000

A CARD FROM 'LILIBET' FOR THE QUEEN MOTHER

KEY EVENTS

In America, after five weeks of uncertainty over the result of the presidential elections, Al Gore conceded victory to George W. Bush.

•••

'A milestone for mankind' followed the announcement that scientists had completed a working draft of the entire human genetic code.

•••

An Air France Concorde crashed near Paris, killing all on board.

•••

In Britain, the Millennium Dome in Greenwich closed on December 31; it had cost about £628 million and had entertained some 6 million customers.

•••

The maverick Labour left-wing MP and former leader of the GLC, Ken Livingstone, was elected the first mayor of London.

•••

The BBC decided not to cover the pageant arranged to celebrate the Queen Mother's birthday. ITV was quick to fill the gap.

•••

Donald Dewar, Scotland's First Minister, died unexpectedly. The Liberal Democrat leader, Jim Wallace, took over until elections could be held, when Henry McLeish became the new First Minister.

*P*rince William celebrated his 18th birthday, the Duke of York his 40th, the Princess Royal her 50th and Princess Margaret her 70th, but all were completely overshadowed by another landmark anniversary: on Friday August 4 Queen Elizabeth, the Queen Mother moved into her own second century and the world wished her the happiest of all birthdays.

Earlier, in July, a service of Thanksgiving for the Queen Mother's life and service, in St Paul's Cathedral, and a quite brilliantly eccentric pageant on Horseguards Parade had, in their very different ways, marked the centenary – and given thousands the chance to join in the fun.

On August 4 itself 40,000 people gathered in the Mall and in the parks round Buckingham Palace to sing and cheer as the Queen Mother came out of Clarence House to take delivery of her card of congratulations from the Queen. She was one of 12 centenarians to whom the Queen had written on that day but her card was the only one signed 'Lilibet'. Opening the envelope proved tricky until her equerry drew his ceremonial sword and slit the envelope open. Minutes later the Queen Mother, with the Prince of Wales beside her, drove to Buckingham Palace in a landau decorated in her racing colours. With her daughters, grandchildren, great-grandchildren and nephews and nieces around her, she stood on the balcony, a small, serene, smiling figure, to acknowledge the thousands who had gathered to wish her well.

In November the Queen Mother had two falls, on the second occasion breaking her collarbone. She had sufficiently recovered, however, to attend church at Sandringham on Christmas morning – against her daughter's advice!

RIGHT It was the Queen Mother's day and, happily, she took centre stage on the Palace balcony.

Prince William 'came of age' in the middle of taking his A-level exams towards the end of his time at Eton. Photographs and videos released at the time revealed a good-looking, appealing young man who had already gained 'brownie points' among his contemporaries by opting not to use the title 'His Royal Highness' until he had finished his education. A 'gap' year was planned before he went up to St. Andrews University in Scotland, and the Prince's 18th birthday was accompanied by appeals from Lord Wakeham, Chairman of the Press Complaints Commission, endorsed by the Palace, that he should continue for the time being to enjoy the freedom from media intrusion that they had accorded him at school. It was a request which met with a positive response. In exchange, the Prince co-operated fully in the film that was made about his experiences with an Operation Raleigh venture in Peru, and many still photographs of his trip were released at the time.

By any measure this Millennium year has been an unforgettable one. Since the turn of the year it has been celebrated and marked in this country and throughout the Commonwealth, and it has been a particular pleasure for me to visit Millennium projects large and small which will be reminders for generations to come of the time when the twenty-first century began.

But as this year draws to a close I would like to reflect more directly and more personally on what lies behind all the celebrations of these past twelve months.

Christmas is the traditional, if not the actual, birthday of a man who was destined to change the course of our history. And today we are celebrating the fact that Jesus Christ was born two thousand years ago; this is the true Millennium anniversary.

The simple facts of Jesus' life give us little clue as to the influence he was to have on the world. As a boy he learnt his father's trade as a carpenter. He then became a preacher, recruiting twelve supporters to help him. But his ministry only lasted a few years and he himself never wrote anything down. In his early thirties he was arrested, tortured and crucified with two criminals. His death might have been the end of the story, but then came the resurrection and with it the foundation of the Christian faith.

Even in our very material age the impact of Christ's life is all around us. If you want to see an expression of Christian faith you have only to look at our awe-inspiring cathedrals and abbeys, listen to their music, or look at their stained glass windows, their books and their pictures.

But the true measure of Christ's influence is not only in the lives of the saints but also in the good works quietly done by millions of men and women day in and day out throughout the centuries.

Many will have been inspired by Jesus' simple but powerful teaching: love God and love thy neighbour as thyself – in other words, treat others as you would like them to treat you. His great emphasis was to give spirituality a practical purpose.

Whether we believe in God or not, I think most of us have a sense of the spiritual, that recognition of a deeper meaning and purpose in our lives, and I believe that this sense flourishes despite the pressures of our world.

This spirituality can be seen in the teaching of other great faiths. Of course, religion can be divisive, but the Bible, the Koran and the sacred texts of the Jews and Hindus, Buddhists and Sikhs, are all sources of divine inspiration and practical guidance passed down through the generations.

To many of us, our beliefs are of fundamental importance. For me the teaching of Christ and my own personal accountability before God provide a framework in which I try to lead my life. I, like so many of you, have drawn great comfort in difficult times from Christ's words and example.

I believe that the Christian message, in the words of a familiar blessing, remains profoundly important to us all:

**'Go forth into the world in peace,
be of good courage,
hold fast that which is good,
render to no man evil for evil,
strengthen the faint-hearted,
support the weak,
help the afflicted,
honour all men.'**

It is a simple message of compassion… and yet as powerful as ever today, two thousand years after Christ's birth.

I hope this day will be as special for you as it is for me. May I wish you all a very Happy Christmas.

The Queen's Christmas Message

It was not the media but Patrick Jephson, a former Private Secretary to Diana, Princess of Wales, from 1988 to 1996, who incurred the wrath of both the Queen and the Prince of Wales. In October he published *Shadows of a Princess*, an 'intimate account', eagerly serialised by *The Sunday Times*. Jephson was accused of breaching an undertaking of confidentiality, and although no legal action was taken against him by either Buckingham Palace or St James's Palace, it was the effect that the book might have on Prince William and Prince Harry that most concerned their father and grandmother.

After the summer break at Balmoral the Queen and Prince Philip paid a state visit to Italy as guests of President Ciampi. It was a successful tour, although once again the Queen and Prince Philip provoked the wrath of extreme Protestants when they spent time with the Pope in Vatican City while they were in Rome. The Queen and the Pope clearly enjoyed meeting each other again after 20 years, and recalling the Pope's visit to Britain.

Earlier in the year the Queen and Prince Philip went to Australia for the first time since the referendum vote for the continuance of the monarchy. There was no sense of triumphalism about the tour and this was noted and appreciated. Throughout, the welcomes were warm and enthusiastic, with republicans seeming anxious to stress that there was nothing personal in the way they had voted..

BELOW *The warmest of welcomes from Australian children as the Queen visited Australia for the first time since the referendum.*

ABOVE *The Queen in the Australian outback town of Bourke, where she met the pupils, their parents, and staff of the local primary school.*

The issue of Civil List allowances cropped up again during the year, and the arrangements agreed between Buckingham Palace and the Government under John Major in 1991 were confirmed for a further 10 years. The reserves built up, as planned, since 1991 had exceeded expectations, and it was agreed that this money (£30 million) would be used to cover any shortfall between the annual Civil List allowances and actual expenditure until 2011. The reconfirmed figures were: an annual allowance of £7.9 million for the Queen as head of state; £643,000 a year for the Queen Mother; and £359,000 a year for Prince Philip. Once again the Prince of Wales was not included; his income comes from the Duchy of Cornwall.

In December the Duke of York announced that in July 2001 he would take early retirement from the Royal Navy, which he had joined in 1979, and take on full-time royal duties with an emphasis on work for British Trade International (BTI). He would be following in the footsteps of the Duke of Kent, who was leaving BTI in April. He had also recently succeeded the Duke as President of the Football Association.

Princess Margaret, who had joined in the summer celebrations, became increasingly unwell towards the end of the year. She was with the family at Sandringham as usual but spent both Christmas and the New Year in bed. She was later taken to the King Edward VII's Hospital for Officers for tests, but was allowed back to Sandringham in the middle of January.

So, for the Queen, with concerns certainly on her mind, there was nevertheless much to recall with genuine pleasure as millennium year came to a close. If she had not been entirely happy at the way in which the year had begun, her Christmas message gave her the opportunity to say clearly and unambiguously what had sustained her, not only in 2000 but in all her years beforehand.

COMMONWEALTH MEMBERS

There are 54 member countries of the Commonwealth. These are listed below, with the years in which they joined the Commonwealth. Also listed is their constitutional status: realm indicates a Commonwealth country which retained a monarchical constitution, recognising The Queen as Sovereign; monarchy indicates an indigenous monarchical constitution.

Country	Date	Status
Antigua and Barbuda	1981	Realm
Australia	1931	Realm
The Bahamas	1973	Realm
Bangladesh	1972	Republic
Barbados	1966	Realm
Belize	1981	Realm
Botswana	1966	Republic
Brunei	1984	Monarchy
Cameroon	1995	Republic
Canada	1931	Realm
Cyprus	1961	Republic
Dominica	1978	Republic
Fiji	1997	Republic
(joined in 1970, left in 1987, rejoined in 1997)		
The Gambia	1965	Republic
Ghana	1957	Republic
Grenada	1974	Realm
Guyana	1966	Republic
India	1947	Republic
Jamaica	1962	Realm
Kenya	1963	Republic
Kiribati	1979	Republic
Lesotho	1966	Monarchy
Malawi	1964	Republic
Malaysia	1957	Monarchy
The Maldives	1982	Republic
Malta	1964	Republic
Mauritius	1968	Republic

Country	Date	Status
Mozambique	1995	Republic
Namibia	1990	Republic
Nauru*	1968	Republic
New Zealand	1931	Realm
Nigeria	1960	Republic
Pakistan	1989	Republic
(joined in 1947, left in 1972, rejoined in 1989)		
Papua New Guinea	1975	Realm
St. Christopher and Nevis	1983	Realm
St. Lucia	1979	Realm
St. Vincent and the Grenadines	1979	Realm
Seychelles	1976	Republic
Sierra Leone	1961	Republic
Singapore	1965	Republic
Solomon Islands	1978	Realm
South Africa	1994	Republic
(joined in 1931, left in 1961, rejoined in 1994)		
Sri Lanka	1948	Republic
Swaziland	1968	Monarchy
Tanzania	1961	Republic
Tonga	1970	Monarchy
Trinidad and Tobago	1962	Republic
Tuvalu*	1978	Realm
United Kingdom		Monarchy
Uganda	1962	Republic
Vanuatu	1980	Republic
Western Samoa	1970	Republic
Zambia	1964	Republic

* Special members, with the right to participate in all functional Commonwealth meetings and activities, but not to attend meetings of Commonwealth Heads of Government.

Countries which have left the Commonwealth
Republic of Ireland (1949)

STATE VISITS PAID BY HM THE QUEEN WITH HRH THE DUKE OF EDINBURGH

1955		
NORWAY	King Haakon VII	June 24–26
1956		
SWEDEN	King Gustaf VI Adolf & Queen Louise	June 8–10
1957		
PORTUGAL	President Craveiro Lopes	February 8–21
FRANCE	President Coty	April 8–11
DENMARK	King Frederik IX & Queen Ingrid	May 21–23
USA	President Eisenhower	Oct 17–21
1958		
NETHERLANDS	Queen Juliana & Prince Bernhard	March 25–27
1961		
NEPAL	King Mahendra & Queen Ratna	Feb 26–March 1
IRAN	Shahansha Mohammad Reza Shah Pahlavi	March 2–6
ITALY	President Gronchi	May 2–5
VATICAN CITY	Pope John XXIII	May 5
LIBERIA	President Tubman	November 23
1965		
ETHIOPIA	Emperor Haile Selassie	February 1–8
SUDAN	President Dr El Tigani El Mahi	February 8–12
FED. REPUBLIC OF GERMANY	President Lübke	May 18–28
1966		
BELGIUM	King Badouin & Queen Fabiola	May 9–13
1968		
BRAZIL	President da Costa e Silva	Nov 5–11
CHILE	President Frei	Nov 11–18
1969		
AUSTRIA	President Jonas	May 5–10
1971		
TURKEY	President Sunay	Oct 18–25
1972		
THAILAND	King Bhumibol & Queen Sirikit	Feb 10–15
MALDIVES	President Nasir	Mar 13–15
FRANCE	President Pompidou	May 15–19
YUGOSLAVIA	President Tito	Oct 17–21
1974		
INDONESIA	President Suharto	Mar 18–22
1975		
MEXICO	President Echeverria Alvarez	Feb 24–March 1
JAPAN	Emperor Hirohito	May 7–12
1976		
FINLAND	President Kekkonen	May 24–28
USA	President Ford	July 6–11
LUXEMBOURG	Grand Duke Jean & Grand Duchess Joséphine Charlotte	Nov 8–12
1978		
FED. REPUBLIC OF GERMANY	President Scheel	May 22–26
1979		
DENMARK	Queen Margrethe II & Prince Henrik	May 16–19
TANZANIA	President Nyerere	July 19–22
MALAWI	President Banda	July 22–25
BOTSWANA	President Seretse Khama	July 25–27
ZAMBIA	President Kaunda	July 27–Aug 4
1980		
SWITZERLAND	President Chevallaz	Apr 29 – May 2
ITALY	President Pertini	Oct 14–20
VATICAN CITY	Pope John Paul II	October 17
TUNISIA	President Bourguiba	Oct 21–23
ALGERIA	President Chadli	Oct 25–27
MOROCCO	King Hassan II	Oct 27–30

1981		
NORWAY	King Olav V	May 5–8
SRI LANKA	President Jayewardene	Oct 21–25
1983		
EDEN	King Carl Gustaf & Queen Silvia	May 25–28
KENYA	President Arap Moi	Nov 10–14
BANGLADESH	President Chowdhury	Nov 14–17
INDIA	President Zail Singh	Nov 17–26
1984		
JORDAN	King Hussein & Queen Noor	Mar 26–30
1985		
PORTUGAL	President & Senhora Eanes	Mar 25–29
1986		
NEPAL	King Birendra & Queen Aishwarya	Feb 17–21
CHINA	President Li Xiannian	Oct 12–18
1988		
SPAIN	King Juan Carlos & Queen Sofia	Oct 17–21
1989		
SINGAPORE	President Wee Kim Wee	Oct 9–11
MALAYSIA	HM The Yang di-Pertuan Agong	
1990		
ICELAND	President Vigdis Finnbogadottir	Jun 25–27
1991		
USA	President Bush	May 14–17
NAMIBIA	President Nujoma	Oct 8–10
ZIMBABWE	President Mugabe	Oct 10–15
1992		
MALTA	President Tabone	May 28–30
FRANCE	President Mitterand	Jun 9–12
GERMANY	President Von Weizsacker	Oct 19–23
1993		
HUNGARY	President Goncz	May 4–7
1994		
RUSSIA	President Yeltsin	Oct 17–20
1995		
SOUTH AFRICA	President Mandela	Mar 19–25
1996		
POLAND	President Walesa	Mar 25–27
CZECH REPUBLIC		
	President Havel	Mar 27–29
THAILAND	King Bhumibol	Oct 28–Nov 1
1997		
PAKISTAN	President Sharma	Oct 6–12
INDIA	President Narayanan	Oct 12–18
1998		
BRUNEI	HM Sultan of Brunei	Sept 17–20
MALAYSIA	HM The Yang di-Pertuan Agong	Sept 20–23
1999		
SOUTH KOREA	President Kim Dae-jung	Apr 19–22
2000		
ITALY	President Ciampi	Oct 16–19
VATICAN CITY (Courtesy call)	Pope John Paul II	Oct 17

In addition the Queen, with the Duke of Edinburgh (and the Duke of Edinburgh on his own account) have paid frequent visits to those Commonwealth countries of which the Queen is Head of State. Republics within the Commonwealth have also been visited on a regular basis.

1954
SWEDEN	King Gustaf VI Adolf & Queen Louise	June 28–July 1
ETHIOPIA	Emperor Haile Selassie	Oct 14–16

1955
PORTUGAL	President Craveiro Lopes	Oct 25–28

1956
IRAQ	King Faisal	July 16–19

1958
ITALY	President Gronchi	May 13–15
FED. REPUBLIC OF GERMANY	President Heuss	Oct 20–23

1959
IRAN	Shahanshah Mohammad Reza Shah Pahlavi	May 5–8

1960
FRANCE	President de Gaulle	April 5–8
THAILAND	King Bhumibol & Queen Sirikit	July 19–21
NEPAL	King Mahendra & Queen Ratna	Oct 17–20

1962
LIBERIA	President Tubman	July 10–13
NORWAY	King Olav V	Oct 16–19

1963
BELGIUM	King Baudouin & Queen Fabiola	May 14–17
GREECE	King Paul & Queen Frederika	July 9–12

1964
SUDAN	President Abbod	May 28–June 3

1965
CHILE	President Frei	July 13–19

1966
AUSTRIA	President Jonas	May 17–21
JORDAN	King Hussein & Princess Muna	July 19–28

1967
SAUDI ARABIA	King Faisal & Queen Iffat	May 9–17
TURKEY	President Sunay	Nov 1–8

1969
ITALY	President Saragat	Apr 22–30
FINLAND	President Kekkonen	Jul 15–18
JAPAN	Emperor Hirohito & Empress Nagako	Oct 5–8

1971
AFGHANISTAN	King Mohammed Zaher Shah	Dec 7–10

1972
NETHERLANDS	Queen Juliana & Prince Bernhard	Apr 11–15
LUXEMBOURG	Grand Duke Jean & Grand Duchess Joséphine Charlotte	June 13–16
FED. REPUBLIC OF GERMANY	President Heinemann	Oct 24–27

1973
MEXICO	President Echeverria Alvarez	Apr 3–6
ZAIRE	President Mobutu	Dec 11–14

1974
DENMARK	Queen Margrethe II & Prince Henrik	Apr 30–May 3
MALAYSIA	HM The Yang di-Pertuan Agong & The Raja Permaisuri Agong	July 9–11

1975
SWEDEN	King Carl XVI Gustaf	July 8–11

1976
BRAZIL	President Geisel	May 4–7
FRANCE	President Giscard d'Estaing	June 22–25

1978
ROMANIA	President Ceauçescu	June 13–16
PORTUGAL	President Eanes	Nov 14–17

1979
KENYA	President Arap Moi	June 12–15
INDONESIA	President Suharto	Nov 13–16

1980
NEPAL	King Birendra & Queen Aishwarya	Nov 18–21

1981
NIGERIA	President Shagari	Mar 17–20
SAUDI ARABIA	King Khalid	June 9–12

1982
OMAN	Qaboos Bin Al Said, Sultan of Oman	Mar 16–19
NETHERLANDS	Queen Beatrix & Prince Claus	Nov 16–19

1983
ZAMBIA	President Kaunda	Mar 22–25

1984
BAHRAIN	Sheikh Isa Bin Sulman Al-Khalifa, Amir of Bahrain	April 10–13
FRANCE	President Mitterand	Oct 22–26

1985
MALAWI	President Dr Banda	April 16–19
MEXICO	President de la Madrid	June 11–14
QATAR	Sheikh Khaifa Bin Hamad Al-Thani, Amir of Qatar	Nov 12–15

1986
SPAIN	King Juan Carlos & Queen Sofia	April 22–25
FED. REPUBLIC OF GERMANY	President Von Weizsäcker	July 1–4

1987
SAUDI ARABIA	King Fahd	Mar 24–27
MOROCCO	King Hassan II	July 14–17

1988
NORWAY	King Olav V	April 12–15
TURKEY	President Evren	July 12–15
SENEGAL	President & Madame Diouf	Nov 8–11

1989
NIGERIA	President & Mrs Babangida	May 9–12
U.A.E.	Sheikh Zayed bin Sultan Al Nahyan	July 18–21

1990
INDIA	President & Shrimali Venkataraman	April 3–6
ITALY	President Cossiga	Oct 23–26

1991
POLAND	President & Mrs Walesa	Apr 23–26
EGYPT	President & Mrs Mubarak	July 23–26

1992
BRUNEI	HM The Sultan of Brunei & The Raja Isteri	Nov 3–6

1993
PORTUGAL	President & Senhora Soares	April 27–30
MALAYSIA	HM The Yang di-Pertuan Agong & The Raja Permaisuri Agong	Nov 9–12

1994
ZIMBABWE	President Mugabe	May 17–20
NORWAY	King Harald & Queen Sonja	July 5–8

1995
KUWAIT	Shaikh Jabir al Ahmed Jabir al Sabah, The Amir	May 23–26
FINLAND	President & Madame Ahtisaari	Oct 17–20

1996
FRANCE	President & Madame Chirac	May 14–17
SOUTH AFRICA	President Mandela	July 9–12

1997
ISRAEL	President & Mrs Weizman	Feb 25–28
BRAZIL	President & Senhora Cardoso	Dec 2–5

1998
JAPAN	Emperor Akihito & Empress Michiko	May 26–29
GERMANY	President & Frau Herzog	Dec 1–4

1999
HUNGARY	President & Mrs Goncz	June 22–25
CHINA	President & Madame Wang Yeping	Oct 19-22

2000
DENMARK	Queen Margrethe II & Prince Henrik	Feb 16-18

HM THE QUEEN'S PRIME MINISTERS

1952 – 1955	Sir Winston Churchill CONSERVATIVE	
1955 – 1957	Sir Anthony Eden CONSERVATIVE	
1957 – 1963	Harold Macmillan CONSERVATIVE	
1963 – 1964	Sir Alec Douglas-Home CONSERVATIVE	
1964 – 1970	Harold Wilson LABOUR	
1970 – 1974	Edward Heath CONSERVATIVE	
1974 – 1976	Harold Wilson LABOUR	
1976 – 1979	James Callaghan LABOUR	
1979 – 1990	Margaret Thatcher CONSERVATIVE	
1990 – 1997	John Major CONSERVATIVE	
1997 –	Tony Blair NEW LABOUR	

THE INDEX

Page numbers in *italics* indicate illustrations. Illustrations of the Queen with other people are normally indexed at the names of those people.

Page numbers in **bold** indicate entries in the main text. Page numbers in roman (i.e. neither in bold nor italics) indicate entries in Key Events listings or in tables.

Victoria
1819–1901
m. Prince Albert of Saxe-Coburg &
Gotha (Prince Consort) (d.1861)

Edward VII
1841–1910
m. Princess Alexandra (1844–1925)

George V
1865–1936
m. Princess Mary (1867–1953)

2 brothers and 3 sisters

Edward VIII
1894–1972
(abdicated 1936; took title of Duke of Windsor)
m. Mrs Wallis Simpson (1896–1986)

George VI
1895–1952
m. Lady Elizabeth Bowes Lyon
(QUEEN ELIZABETH The Queen Mother)

Mary,
Princess Royal
1897–1965
m. 6th Earl of Harewood

2 sons

Elizabeth II
b. 1926
m. Philip, DUKE OF EDINBURGH

Princess Margaret
b. 1930
m. Antony Armstrong-Jones, EARL OF SNOWDON

David,
Viscount Linley
b. 1961
m. Serena Stanhope

Lady Sarah Armstrong-Jones
b. 1964
m. Daniel Chatto

Hon. Charles Linley
b. 1999

Samuel Chatto
b. 1996

Arthur Chatto
b. 1999

Charles,
Prince of Wales
b. 1948
m. Lady Diana Spencer
(divorced 1996)
(d.1997)

Anne,
The Princess Royal
b. 1950
m. Captain Mark Phillips
(divorced 1992)
m. Commander Timothy Laurence

Andrew,
Duke of York
b. 1960
m. Sarah Ferguson
(divorced 1996)

Edward,
Earl of Wessex
b. 1964
m. Sophie Rhys-Jones

Peter Phillips
b. 1977

Zara Phillips
b. 1981

Prince William of Wales
b. 1982

Prince Henry of Wales
b. 1984

Princess Beatrice of York
b. 1988

Princess Eugenie of York
b. 1990